California
Government

California Government

Fourth Edition

John L. Korey
California State Polytechnic University, Pomona

Houghton Mifflin Company   Boston   New York

DEDICATION

To Mary, always
and to the newest family members—
Welcome to California

Publisher: Charles Hartford
Sponsoring Editor: Katherine Meisenheimer
Assistant Editor: Christina Lembo
Editorial Assistant: Kristen Craib
Associate Project Editor: Teresa Huang
Editorial Assistant: Jake Perry
Senior Art and Design Coordinator: Jill Haber
Senior Photo Editor: Jennifer Meyer Dare
Senior Composition Buyer: Sarah Ambrose
Manufacturing Coordinator: Carrie Wagner
Executive Marketing Manager: Nicola Poser
Marketing Associate: Kathleen Mellon

Cover image: Primary California Photography, © Harold Burch, New York City. California State Bear Photo © Bob Rowan, Progressive Image/CORBIS.

Printed in the U.S.A.

Library of Congress Control Number: 2003116166

ISBN: 0-618-45234-6

3456789-QF-10 09 08 07 06

Contents

★ ★ ★ ★ ★ ★ ★ ★ ★

Preface

*W*hen our daughter, Meghan, was a little girl, she went to visit relatives on the East Coast. While playing with friends, she drew a small butterfly on her knee, and convinced her playmates that this was a big fad in California. Soon, this "fad" spread among the other children. Meghan had caught on early to the Golden State's cutting edge reputation, which has earned the fascination, though not always the admiration, of the rest of the country.

In politics as well as culture, California can be just different enough to be confusing. Understanding the differences and the similarities is especially important given California's emphasis on direct democracy, which places especially high demands on citizens to act in an informed way. It remains the goal of this edition to help readers do so.

The new edition retains the conciseness and clarity of the first three. Like previous editions, this fourth edition goes beyond description of the formal structures of politics and focuses on how people actually engage in political activity. Where necessary, I have undertaken original research to fill gaps in available information.

REVISIONS

The basic structure of the fourth edition resembles that of the third. All chapters have been thoroughly updated, and several have been significantly reworked. Chapters 2 and 9, for example, provide expanded analysis of the recall of state and local officials, respectively. Chapter 5 includes a new section on declining voter turnout. Chapter 8 contains new material on voting alignments within the state supreme court and on the criminal justice system. Chapter 9 contains a new section on Native American tribes and their role in state politics.

HELP FOR STUDENTS

Glossary.   Key terms that are either specific to or especially important in California politics are indicated in boldface when they first appear in the text (except when mentioned incidentally). A glossary of these terms is provided in the back of the book.

Surfing California: Internet Resources.   Each chapter ends with a set of suggestions and URLs for students to use in exploring California politics on the world wide web. In addition, the Houghton Mifflin College Division Web site (at college.hmco.com) includes an expanded book companion site where students will find chapter summaries, updates explaining changes that have taken place in the political process, updated chapter links, and sample test questions.

HELP FOR INSTRUCTORS

The expanded book Web site at college.hmco.com also contains ancillary material for instructors, including the following:

Test Item File.   Instructors adopting *California Government* can obtain the password to access this online resource by contacting their Houghton Mifflin campus sales representative.

Lecture Resources.   These include PowerPoint™ presentations, essays providing in-depth analysis of selected topics, and links to Internet materials useful for faculty research.

ACKNOWLEDGMENTS

I remain in the debt of all whose contributions were acknowledged in the first three editions. Doug Glaeser was particularly generous in guiding me through the constitutional issues addressed in Chapter 8. The reviewers for this edition contributed a number of insightful suggestions—Scott C. Heffner, De Anza College; James J. Kelleher, College of the Canyons; and Steven Holmes, Bakersfield College. I'd also like to thank the editors at Houghton Mifflin—Katherine Meisenheimer, Christina Lembo, and Teresa Huang—for their professionalism and their patience. Richard Stephens read the entire work and significantly improved its clarity and style, as did my wife, Mary Haggerty Korey. Michael Hout generously shared his analysis of ideological differences between Californians and residents of other states described in Chapter 3. Charles Gossett, Mark Schmuck, and Mark Lukasik shared their expertise regarding tribal governments, the courts, and the criminal justice system, respectively. Field Poll data were provided through the Social Science Data Base Archive at California State University, Los Angeles.

J. L. K.

California
Government

1. *"America, Only More So"*[1]

What happens here happens five years before anywhere else in America.
—HARLAN ELLISON[2]

*F*or better and for worse, Californians tend to *think* they are different. When asked in a Fall 2000 Field Poll[3] whether they thought that they were "fundamentally different" from other Americans, almost half of those surveyed thought that they were, while only a third thought that they were not. Californians' self-image was generally but not completely favorable. Specifically, a majority thought that Californians were "trendier," more "diverse," more "enterprising," more "health-conscious," more "tolerant/open-minded," more "money-oriented," and less "old fashioned." Respondents were also more likely (although there were no majorities on either side) to see Californians as "self-indulgent," "fun loving," "arrogant," and "dishonest" and less "God fearing" and less "family-oriented."

The state has long enjoyed and suffered an image of being on the cutting edge of change: a place in which trends originate before spreading to the rest of the country. Whether this will continue to be true in the new century is the subject of some controversy. A few years ago, the authors of the respected *Almanac of American Politics* wrote that "it is uncertain whether [California] is still the harbinger of the future it has been for most of the last half of the twentieth century."[4] One article about the state was headlined, "California Doesn't Matter: The Political Future Once Happened There; No More."[5] Another article, however, rejected this conclusion, arguing that America as a whole still "shows every sign of following California's culture and politics."[6]

CALIFORNIA AND THE NATION

Part of this debate revolves around the question of the extent to which California has become a different sort of place from the rest of the country. The "California lifestyle" is often stereotyped, but there are some ways—both good and bad—in which the state is in fact distinctive. It is in certain respects a very health-conscious place, ranking second in the

1

nation in seat-belt use and next to last (ahead of Utah) in the proportion of the population who are smokers. This concern for one's own health does not necessarily extend to concern for the health of others: California's rate of violent crime in 2002 was 20 percent above that of the nation as a whole.[7]

Economically, the gap between the rich and poor is significantly greater in California and has been growing at a more rapid rate at least since the latter part of the 1960s.[8] In the 2000 census, California was tied for fifth for the most unequal income distribution among households.[9] Overall, California's economy has undergone dramatic change in recent years. With the end of the Cold War, the state, heavily reliant on the defense and aerospace industries, was hit especially hard by the recession of the early 1990s. By mid-decade, California had rebounded, in part by becoming a national and world leader in "new economy" fields such as information and biotechnology. The new prosperity, however, brought new problems. For example, a bourgeoning population of the newly well-to-do in Silicon Valley and other areas (mostly near the coast) caused housing prices to sky-rocket. (In 2002, the median value of owner-occupied housing stood at $275,526, double the national figure.[10]) This forced many lower-income workers to move inland and endure seemingly interminable commutes to work.[11] Shortly after the start of the new century, the state's economy again faltered, partly due to nationwide trends, but also as a consequence of the bursting of the dot.com bubble, and an energy crisis that rocked California in 2001. As of this writing, the roller-coaster ride seems to be continuing, since most economic indicators have again turned positive.

In politics, California has shown an increasing tendency in recent years to favor the Democratic Party. In each of the last six presidential elections, the Democratic candidate has done better in California than in the rest of the country. This difference reached a peak in 2000, when Democrat Al Gore led Republican George W. Bush by almost 12 percentage points in the popular vote in California, compared to his approximately one-half point lead in the nation as a whole. In 2004, John Kerry, despite losing the popular vote nationwide by about three percentage points, bested Bush in California by a margin only slightly smaller than Gore's four years earlier. Democrats also have come to dominate elected offices at the state level. Democrats in 2004 held seven of the eight statewide elected positions[12] and enjoyed substantial majorities in both chambers of the state legislature. It remains to be seen whether the election of Republican Governor Arnold Schwarzenegger in 2003 portends a new trend or just a temporary reversal of the parties' fortunes.

POPULATION TRENDS

The most obvious way in which California is different is the size of its population; its status as the most populous state is critical to its prominence in national politics. When it became a state in 1850, California had a population of less than 93,000, less than 0.5 percent of the nation's total.[13] By the 2000 census, almost 34 million people, 12 percent of all Americans, called California home. As a result, California has the largest contingents, and potentially the most clout, in the U.S. House of Representatives and in the electoral college (which chooses the president of the United States). California currently holds 53 seats in the 435-member House and casts a bloc of 55 electoral college votes out of a total of 538.

California has not only the largest population of any state but also the most ethnically diverse. Over 40 percent of Californians speak a language other than English at home, a figure well above that of any other state and more than double the figure for the country as a whole.[14]

Table 1.1 shows a breakdown by ethnicity of the population in 2000 for California and for the United States as a whole.[15] Anglos, who made up almost three-quarters of the nation's population, were less than half of the population of California, making this state (along with Hawaii and New Mexico) one of only three "minority-majority" states. Like Anglos, African Americans are a smaller proportion of the population in California than in the United States as a whole. Whereas about one of every eight Americans is an African American, the same is true of only about one in every sixteen Californians. Latinos and Asian Americans, on the other hand, are represented in California at about three times the national rate. In fact, about 31 percent of all Latinos in the United States and about 36 percent of all Asian Americans live in California. Native Americans make up less than 1 percent of both the U.S. and California populations.

Figure 1.1 shows population estimates for California through 2050.[16] According to the estimates, Latinos will become the state's largest ethnic group by around 2010 and by midcentury will account for more than half of the state's residents. Anglos, currently almost half of the state's population, are projected to drop to below one-fourth by 2050. As a percentage of total population, the figures for other groups are not expected to change dramatically. (Native Americans are expected to grow at the fastest *rate* of all

---

TABLE 1.1
Ethnicity: California and the Nation

	California		U.S.	
	Millions of people	Percent	Millions of people	Percent
Anglo	15.8	47	194.6	69
Latino*	11.0	32	35.3	13
Asian/Pacific Islander	3.8	11	10.5	4
African American	2.2	6	33.9	12
Native American	0.2	1	2.1	1
Other/More than one	1.0	3	5.1	2
	33.9	100	281.4	100

*Latinos may be of any race.
SOURCE: California Department of Finance, "Population Projections by Race/Ethnicity, Gender and Age for California and Its Counties 2000–2050," Sacramento, California, May 2004.

FIGURE 1.1
Projected Ethnic Distribution of California Population, 2000–2050

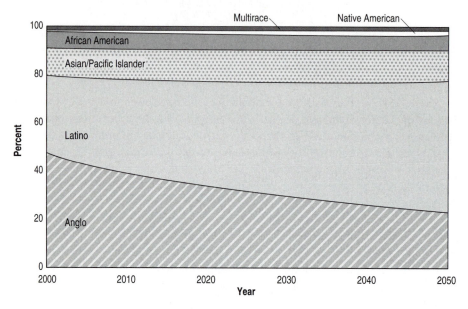

SOURCE: California Department of Finance, "Population Projections by Race/Ethnicity, Gender and Age for California and Its Counties 2000–2050," Sacramento, California, May 2004.

groups, but to still make up only a small *proportion* of total population.) As we will see at several points throughout this text, California's changing demographics are already having a profound impact on its politics.

Figure 1.1 should come with several qualifications. First, projections going forward almost a half century are certain to prove inaccurate in important respects as the result of developments, both domestic and international, that are impossible to predict. One comparison of several population projections showed that estimates of the state's total population in 2025 ranged from a low of 41.5 million to a high of 51.8 million, with considerable variation in the projected growth rates of different ethnic groups.[17] Second, even if the numbers should turn out to be approximately correct, their social and political meanings are likely to change. After all, German, Irish, Italian, and various other Americans who are now generally regarded as part of the "Anglo" majority were once considered what today are called "ethnic minorities."

Finally, dividing people into ethnic groupings, as we have done here, may hide more than it reveals. Each of the categories in Table 1.1 and Figure 1.1 includes various subcategories. To give just one example, although both are classified as Asian Americans, Japanese Americans tend to be quite different from Korean Americans in political attitudes and behavior.[18] Moreover, ethnicity is only one of a myriad of factors that help make us who we are; other factors include age, class, gender, occupation, marital status,

These sixth graders at a school in Sacramento reflect the state's growing racial and ethnic diversity. *(© Lynsey Addario/CORBIS SABA)*

length of time our families have lived in the United States, religion, and sexual orientation, as well as the various personality traits and experiences unique to each individual. From time to time in the course of this book, we will make certain generalizations about the impact of people's ethnicity on their politics, but these will be just that, generalizations.

DEMOCRACY, CALIFORNIA STYLE

In broad outline, the government of the state of California resembles the federal government. To mention just some of the similarities, the same two parties, Democrats and Republicans, dominate both levels of government; both state and nation are governed under constitutions providing for the separation of powers among legislative, executive, and judicial branches; both Congress and the California state legislature are bicameral (that is, divided into two chambers); most federal and state employees work under civil service systems; both levels of government have court systems headed by "supreme" courts. Throughout this text, we will tend to focus on some of the differences between the two systems, but this focus should not obscure the far more basic similarities.

Chapter 2 will discuss the state constitution, a radically different sort of document from the U.S. Constitution. It is far longer and far more specific about the powers, structure, and operations of government; it goes into far greater detail in prescribing public policy; and it is far easier to amend. Also, whereas the U.S. Constitution provides that decisions about public policy be made by officials *representing* the people, the state constitution adds to representative democracy an overlay of *direct* democracy, through which the people can themselves vote on policy questions.

Chapter 3 will focus on public opinion and the media. For the most part, patterns of public opinion in California are similar to those in the rest of the country—Californians have political views not radically different from those of their fellow Americans, although there is evidence that Californians tend to be somewhat more liberal on a range of issues. Two patterns, however, deserve special attention in the California context. The first is regional differences within the state. These have traditionally been described as differences between northern and southern California. Careful examination, however, shows that regional differences come closer to being coast versus interior rather than north versus south. The second pattern that needs special attention in the California context is the complex relationship between opinion and ethnicity.

Chapter 3 will also cover the somewhat paradoxical role of the media. On the one hand, California is highly dependent on mass media, and events in the state—from natural disasters to sensational murder trials—are the focus of intense interest, not only in the state but throughout the country. On the other hand, except for major elections and periodic crises, state government receives little in-depth coverage. The local governments of all but the largest cities and counties receive even less attention.

Ever since the Progressive Era early in the twentieth century, California has had a reputation as a state with weak political parties and strong interest groups. Although interest groups remain strong and parties *as organizations* continue to be limited, both by state law and the low public esteem in which they are held, there are sharp differences between Democrats and Republicans among voters and, even more so, among elected officials. The roles of political parties and interest groups in California politics, including the recent experiment with blanket primaries (in which a voter could vote without regard to his or her party affiliation), will be described in Chapter 4.

Chapter 5 will be devoted to an explanation of campaigns and elections. In addition to setting forth the formal rules governing these subjects, the chapter will devote particular attention to voting patterns, including the growth of absentee voting, declining voter turnout, and the roles of campaign finance and of campaign-management firms.

Chapters 6 through 8 will cover, respectively, the legislative, executive, and judicial branches of state government. The basic structure and function of the state legislature are similar to those of the U.S. Congress. There are, however, significant differences in such matters as size, voting procedures, and leadership roles. Chapter 6 will explore these differences and will, among other things, discuss the way in which legislative district boundary lines are drawn and the impact that term limits have had on career patterns. It will also compare how Republican and Democratic lawmakers vote on legislation.

Chapter 7 will examine the executive branch of state government. In contrast to the national government, which has only two elected executives, the president and the vice president (both chosen on the same party ticket), California state government has a "plural" executive. It includes eight statewide executives (governor, lieutenant governor, attorney general, secretary of state, insurance commissioner, superintendent of public instruction, treasurer, and controller) plus four members of the Board of Equalization chosen regionally. Each of these executives is elected directly by the voters. Chapter 7 will describe each of these offices and will also explain how the administration of state government is organized.

Chapter 8 turns to the state's judicial process. Like the federal judiciary, the state court system can be described in general terms as divided into local trial courts, intermediate courts of appeals, and a high, or supreme, court. The state and federal systems do differ in a number of ways, perhaps most importantly in the way in which judges are selected, with the state system giving voters some direct say in the process. Chapter 8 will also describe recent voting alignments on the state supreme court and will explain the relationship between the state and the federal judicial systems through a discussion of the "independent grounds" doctrine of constitutional interpretation. The state's corrections system will be described as well.

In addition to their state government, Californians are served and ruled by the governments of 58 counties, 476 cities (San Francisco counts as both a city and county), about a thousand school districts, and close to five thousand special districts. Chapter 9 will describe what these governing entities do and how they are structured, and will also take a look at California's Native American tribal governments and their growing impact on state politics.

Finally, Chapter 10 will examine government finance in California. It will look at where the government's money (local as well as state) comes from, where it goes, and how decisions on taxing and spending are made. Recent trends in state and local budgeting will be reviewed.

SURFING CALIFORNIA: INTERNET RESOURCES

Most of the more interesting Web sites dealing with California government and politics are specific to topics covered in later chapters. At the end of each chapter you will find the relevant addresses listed and described. Here, however, are a few general ones that are useful.

The official California home page is at:

http://www.ca.gov

Other good sites include:

California Voter Foundation, *Links*:

http://www.calvoter.org/links.html

The Library of Congress, *California State and Local Government*:
http://lcweb.loc.gov/global/state/ca-gov.html

Piper Communications, *California State and Local Government*:
http://www.statelocalgov.net/state-ca.htm

Institute of Government Studies Library, University of California, Berkeley, *California Government and Public Policy Internet Resources*:
http://www.igs.berkeley.edu/library/gallery-ca.html

The University Library, University of California, Davis, *State and Local Governments:*
http://old.lib.ucdavis.edu/govdoc/State/

For involvement opportunities in politics and government, see
http://www.class.csupomona.edu/pls/involve.htm

2. The State Constitution and Direct Democracy

[The U.S. Constitution is] the written embodiment of our freedoms, our rights, and the rule of law.
—ROBERT WEISSBERG[1]

[The California Constitution is] a massive mishmash of minutiae.
—GEORGE SKELTON[2]

Most American government textbooks include the full text of the U.S. Constitution in an appendix. Note that the constitution of the state of California is *not* appended to this text—if it were, the book would be about twice its current length.

A DIFFERENT SORT OF DOCUMENT

The U.S. Constitution (with amendments appended to the original) is 30 pages long, while the California document (with amendments integrated into the text) runs 157 pages.[3] The reason for this difference in length is that the federal constitution spells out the structure of government and the rights of citizens in mostly very general terms and says very little at all about substantive public policy. The state constitution, on the other hand, is much more than a general outline of California's political system. Compare the list of articles in the U.S. Constitution with that for the California Constitution (see Table 2.1). Many of the provisions in the latter document dealing with such matters as water resources, labor relations, and usury (excessive interest rates) are extremely specific. For example, an amendment adopted in 1990 to outlaw gill-net fishing provided a precise fee schedule for permits issued during a three-year phaseout period.[4]

HISTORICAL BACKGROUND

The state's first constitution was adopted in 1849, the year before California gained statehood. Relatively brief,[5] it was approved by a popular vote of 12,061 to 811 after being drafted at a convention in Monterey.[6] It was amended only three times during the thirty

TABLE 2.1
Articles in the United States and the California Constitutions

United States Constitution	California Constitution
Legislative	Declaration of Rights
Executive	Voting, Initiative and Referendum, and Recall
Judicial	State of California
Federalism	Legislative
Amendments	Executive
Miscellaneous Subjects	Judicial
Ratification	Public Officers and Employees
	Education
	Water
	Local Government
	Public Utilities
	Taxation
	Labor Relations
	Usury
	Public Finance
	Amending and Revising the Constitution
	Motor Vehicle Revenues
	Miscellaneous Subjects
	Reapportionment of the Senate, Assembly, Congressional, and Board of Equalization Districts
	Public Housing Project Law

years of its existence. This may have been due less to satisfaction with the document than to the difficulty of the amendment process.[7] There were several unsuccessful attempts, the earliest in 1857, to call a convention to write a new constitution.[8]

Unrest grew during the 1870s. Many small farmers were deeply in debt and heavily taxed. Business failures late in the decade led to growing unemployment in the cities. A relatively small number of people owned much of the state's manufacturing. In particular, the power of the railroads over both manufacturing and agriculture was deeply resented. Many people held officeholders in extremely low regard. Years later, writing about politicians of this era, Carl Swisher remarked that they were generally "of mediocre talent and often of doubtful integrity. The legislators were of especially low caliber,"[9] and quoted British observer James Bryce, who had remarked that "those who had virtue enough not to be 'got at' by the great corporations, had not intelligence enough to know how to resist their devices."[10]

The Workingman's Party of California was formed in response to these conditions. The party's leader was Dennis Kearney. He was the best known of the "sandlotters," fiery speakers who would gather crowds in vacant lots to give voice to the growing anger and frustration many felt. Kearney bitterly attacked big business, but he reserved much of his venom for Chinese laborers who had been brought to California to work at extremely low wages. Agitation by Kearney and his followers, and by disgruntled farmers, led to a new constitutional convention in late 1878. The convention completed its work early the following year, and on May 7, 1879, a new constitution was ratified by the voters.

The convention accomplished little that those who had pressed for it had hoped. Farmers and workers were well represented at the convention, but they were often outmaneuvered by business people and their lawyers.[11] Much of what the delegates did succeed in including in the constitution would have little real impact afterward. Fortunately, provisions to exclude Chinese immigrants were invalidated in federal court in 1880 because they violated both the Fourteenth Amendment of the U.S. Constitution and treaty obligations with China.[12] Railroads and other large corporations successfully used lawsuits to thwart the taxes the new constitution had imposed on them. A commission was established to regulate the railroads, but it quickly fell under the control of the railroads themselves.[13]

The convention did succeed in producing what has been called "a document that was the perfect example of what a constitution ought *not* to be."[14] It was cluttered with details that would have been left to the ordinary legislative process, if the delegates had trusted present or future legislatures.

Many of the problems that led to the convention would remain for the **Progressives** to try to resolve a generation later.[15] The underlying problem, as the Progressives saw it, was that popular control over government was weak because it was indirect. Their answer was to weaken intervening institutions, especially political parties, and give power directly to the people. A coalition of Progressives from both parties won a majority in the state legislature and elected Republican Hiram Johnson as governor in 1910. They went on to alter the state's constitution fundamentally. Despite a number of important changes that have taken place since, the basic framework of California government today was in place by the time the Progressives had finished their work. Along with other innovations, such as the primary, discussed in Chapter 5, their legacy included most of the elements of "direct democracy" described in the next section.

DIRECT DEMOCRACY

In *Federalist Paper* No. 10, written in 1787 to support ratification of the Constitution of the United States, James Madison argued the advantages of a republic over a pure democracy. By "pure democracy," he meant what today we call a **direct democracy**, a system in which the people themselves decide what public policy should be. By a "republic" he meant what today we more commonly call a **representative democracy**, a system in which such decisions are made, not by the people themselves, but through representatives the people choose to act on their behalf. The U.S. Constitution was designed to provide representative rather than direct democracy. At the national level, the Constitution guarantees citizens the right to "petition the government for redress of grievances," but new legislation can be formally introduced only by a member of Congress. Measures approved by Congress and (usually) the president do not have to be ratified by popular vote to become law. If citizens do not like the way that their elected representatives are acting, there is nothing in the Constitution allowing them to "throw the rascals out" prior to the end of their terms.

In state and local politics in California, however, the people have access to powerful instruments of government not found at the federal level: the **initiative,** the **referendum,** and the **recall.** We will describe each of these in turn as they impact state government generally, and then discuss how the first two have been used to alter the state constitution. Direct democracy at the local level will be addressed in Chapter 9.

The Initiative[16]

California, which adopted the practice in 1911, is one of twenty-four states that provide for some form of statewide initiative.[17] The initiative (called that because it is "initiated" by voter petition) is the purest form of direct democracy. Through it, Californians can write laws, and even amend the state constitution, without having to go through the state legislature. Placing a **proposition** on the ballot for voter approval requires a petition signed by a number of registered voters equal to 5 percent of the number of votes cast in the most recent election for governor (if the measure is an ordinary statute) or 8 percent of this number (if it is a constitutional amendment). The legislature may amend or repeal a statute initiative, but any such change must be approved by the voters unless the initiative itself specifies otherwise. Initiatives must be confined to a "single subject," a concept that will be discussed more fully later in this chapter.

The Referendum[18]

The referendum (called that because it is "referred" to the voters by the legislature) predates the Progressive Era. There are two types of referendums, the **compulsory referendum** and the **petition referendum.**

Referendums are compulsory for constitutional amendments and for the issuance of most government bonds. In order to become ballot propositions, statewide compulsory referendums must first be approved in both the senate and the assembly by a two-thirds vote of the membership.

If voters are unhappy with a statute passed by the legislature, they can in most cases file petitions within 90 days asking that it be referred to the voters for approval before becoming law. The requirement for a petition referendum is the same as for a statute initiative: a number of signatures equaling 5 percent of the number of voters in the last contest for governor. Petition referendums are fairly infrequent. A total of 43 have appeared on the ballot. Of these, however, only 15 have won voter endorsement. In other words, voters have opted to overrule the legislature in most cases.[19] In March 2000, voters rejected two statutes and approved a third that dealt with casino gambling on tribal lands. In November 2004, voters rejected a statute requiring most businesses to provide medical insurance to their employees.

Once on the ballot, a simple majority of votes is all that is needed for passage of either an initiative or a referendum. If two or more conflicting propositions (referendum or initiative, or both) appear on the ballot at the same time and both are approved, the one passing with the highest number of Yes votes will prevail.[20]

STATE MEASURES

64	**LIMITS ON PRIVATE ENFORCEMENT OF UNFAIR BUSINESS COMPETITION LAWS. INITIATIVE STATUTE.** Allows individual or class action "unfair business" lawsuits only if actual loss suffered; only	**106**	**YES ➡ ○**
		107	**NO ➡ ○**

government officials may enforce these laws on public's behalf. Fiscal Impact: Unknown state fiscal impact depending on whether the measure increases or decreases court workload and the extent to which diverted funds are replaced. Unknown potential costs to local governments, depending on the extent to which diverted funds are replaced.

65	**LOCAL GOVERNMENT FUNDS, REVENUES. STATE MANDATES. INITIATIVE CONSTITUTIONAL AMENDMENT.** Requires voter approval for reduction of local fee/tax revenues.	**110**	**YES ➡ ○**
		111	**NO ➡ ○**

Permits suspension of state mandate if no state reimbursement to local government within 180 days after obligation determined. Fiscal Impact: Higher local government revenues than otherwise would have been the case, possibly in the billions of dollars annually over time. Any such local revenue impacts would result in decreased resources to the state of similar amounts.

66	**LIMITATIONS ON "THREE STRIKES" LAW. SEX CRIMES. PUNISHMENT. INITIATIVE STATUTE.** Limits "Three Strikes" law to violent and/or serious felonies. Permits limited resentencing under new	**114**	**YES ➡ ○**
		115	**NO ➡ ○**

definitions. Increases punishment for specified sex crimes against children. Fiscal Impact: Over the long run, net state savings of up to several hundred million dollars annually, primarily to the prison system; local jail and court–related costs of potentially more than ten million dollars annually.

67	**EMERGENCY MEDICAL SERVICES. FUNDING. TELEPHONE SURCHARGE. INITIATIVE CONSTITUTIONAL AMENDMENT AND STATUTE.** Increases telephone surcharge and allocates other	**117**	**YES ➡ ○**
		118	**NO ➡ ○**

funds for emergency room physicians, hospital emergency rooms, community clinics, emergency personnel training/equipment, and 911 telephone system. Fiscal Impact: Increased state revenues of about $500 million annually to reimburse physicians and hospitals for uncompensated emergency medical services and other specified purposes. Continues $32 million in state funding for physicians and clinics for uncompensated medical care.

68	**NON–TRIBAL COMMERCIAL GAMBLING EXPANSION. TRIBAL GAMING COMPACT AMENDMENTS. REVENUES, TAX EXEMPTIONS. INITIATIVE CONSTITUTIONAL AMENDMENT**	**121**	**YES ➡ ○**
		122	**NO ➡ ○**

AND STATUTE. Authorizes tribal compact amendments. Unless tribes accept, authorizes casino gaming for sixteen non–tribal establishments. Percentage of gaming revenues fund government services. Fiscal Impact: Increased gambling revenues–potentially over $1 billion annually–primarily to local governments for additional specified services. Depending on outcome of tribal negotiations, potential loss of state revenues totaling hundreds of millions of dollars annually.

69	**DNA SAMPLES. COLLECTION. DATABASE. FUNDING. INITIATIVE STATUTE.** Requires collection of DNA samples from all felons, and from others arrested for or charged with specified crimes,	**125**	**YES ➡ ○**
		126	**NO ➡ ○**

and submission to state DNA database. Provides for funding. Fiscal Impact: Net state cost to process DNA samples of potentially nearly $20 million annually when costs are fully realized. Local costs likely more than fully offset by revenues, with the additional revenues available for other DNA–related activities.

CONTINUE VOTING ON NEXT PAGE

05-001E

N LA 249-009

In addition to choosing a variety of elected officeholders, Californians also vote to approve or disapprove referendums and initiatives. The measures shown here are among the 16 statewide propositions that appeared on the November 2004 ballot.

All states except Delaware have the referendum in some form as a means of amending the state constitution. Twenty-four provide for the petition referendum.[21]

Together, the referendum and the initiative have helped make for some very long ballots. This was especially true in March 2000, when voters had to deal with twenty statewide propositions. Figure 2.1 shows the total number of measures appearing on the ballot in each decade since the adoption of the constitution. The highest levels were established during the Progressive Era and the decades immediately following it, and in the last decades of the twentieth century. Although the current decade is only half over, the number of propositions that have appeared so far do not seem unusually high by historical standards.[22]

The Recall[23]

The recall, adopted by California state government in 1911, allows voters to remove an elected official before the end of the official's term of office. Including California, eighteen states provide for the recall of at least some state officeholders.[24] Qualifying a recall election of a governor or other statewide office holder requires a number of signatures equal to 12 percent of the number of votes cast in the most recent election for the office involved. For other state office holders (state legislators, members of the Board of Equalization, and appellate and trial court judges), the requirement is 20 percent.

FIGURE 2.1
Ballot Measures (Propositions) by Decade

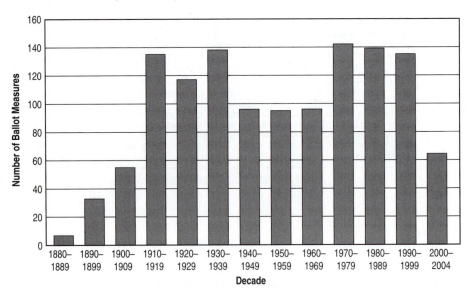

SOURCE: Through 1993: Tony Miller, *A Study of California Ballot Measures 1884–1993* (Sacramento: Secretary of State, 1994); 1994–1996: Statement of Vote; 1998–present: *http://ss.ca.gov/*.

Note that a recall differs from impeachment and removal from office by the legislature, not only because it is carried out by the voters themselves, but also because impeachment requires that an official must have engaged in "misconduct in office."[25] This term is vague enough, but any grounds at all will do for a recall. In fact, the state constitution specifically stipulates that "sufficiency of reason is not reviewable."

If a recall qualifies for the ballot, voters are then asked to decide two questions. The first is, "Shall _____ be recalled (removed) from the office of _____?" The second is who should replace the incumbent if the recall is successful. The first question is decided by a simple majority. The second is decided by a plurality—whoever receives more votes than anyone else (not necessarily a majority of votes cast) wins the office. The incumbent is not permitted to be a candidate on the replacement portion of the ballot.

Until 2003, no statewide officeholder had ever been recalled in California. Only seven attempts, all against members of the state legislature, had qualified for the ballot. Four of these succeeded. Despite 31 attempts, no measure to recall a governor had ever qualified for the ballot.[26] All of this changed with the recall of Gray Davis and his replacement by Arnold Schwarzenegger on October 7, 2003.

First elected as governor in 1998, Davis, a Democrat, enjoyed early success as the state's economy boomed and as his party increasingly dominated state politics. After 2000, however, he suffered a series of reversals, including a severe energy crisis, a faltering economy, and budgetary deficits and gridlock. By midsummer of 2003, his job approval rating, according to the Field Poll, had sunk to 22 percent, the lowest rating for any governor in the many years that this poll had been measuring gubernatorial performance.[27]

As the filing deadline for the recall election approached, it seemed to most observers that Schwarzenegger, a Republican, would decline to run. He was expected to announce this decision at an appearance on Jay Leno's *Tonight* show. Instead, he shocked almost everyone by declaring that he would, in fact, be a candidate.

In the end, the election was a decisive rejection of Davis and a stunning victory for Schwarzenegger. The recall was favored by a margin of 55 to 45. On the replacement portion of the ballot, Schwarzenegger received 49 percent of the vote, with Democratic Lieutenant Governor Cruz Bustamante coming in second at 31 percent, and Republican State Senator Tom McClintock third at 13 percent.[28]

Exit polls[29] showed the breadth of Schwarzenegger's victory. He led the field in all age categories, among both men and women, and among conservatives and moderates (although not among liberals). He outpolled the more conservative McClintock by a huge margin among Republicans, and he even did respectably well among Latinos, with almost a third of the vote (versus a little over half for Bustamante).

CHANGING THE CONSTITUTION

We have already discussed the initiative and referendum in general. Here, we will look more specifically at how they have been used to alter the state constitution. (The constitution can also be revised by a convention,[30] but none has been called since adoption of the current document.) In addition to being limited (as noted earlier) to a single subject, an initiative can only amend, but cannot revise, the state constitution.[31] Unfortunately, the constitution defines neither the term "single subject" nor the distinction between an amendment and a revision. In practice, these provisions have seldom proven to be major limitations on initiatives, some of which have been quite broad. Only twice, in 1948 and again in 1990, has the state supreme court invalidated an initiative on the grounds that it represented a revision.[32] The high court had never thrown out an initiative (either a statute or a constitutional amendment) for violating the single-subject rule until 2000, when it ordered Proposition 24 (which dealt with both reapportionment and legislative salaries) removed from the ballot.[33]

Referendums may either revise or amend the constitution, and are not subject to the single-subject requirement. The constitution does require that when the legislature refers amendments to the voters, "[e]ach amendment shall be so prepared that it can be voted on separately."[34] In 2004, the Third District Court of Appeals ruled that a referendum changing the state primary and providing for sale of surplus state property constituted two different amendments, rejected the contention that grouping unrelated amendments together constituted a revision, and ordered the secretary of state to divide the proposal into two separate ballot measures.[35] In the end, the court's action made no difference, as both measures passed.

In the roughly 125 years of its existence, the California Constitution has been altered over 500 times, more times than any other state constitution.[36] The great majority of these changes (through November 2004, 471 of 514) have come about through the referendum. Moreover, voters are much more likely to approve referendum measures than initiatives. Almost two-thirds of the amendments the legislature has placed on the ballot have been successful, compared to about a third of those placed on the ballot by petition.

It is far easier to alter the California than the federal constitution (which in well over 200 years has been amended only 27 times). Given the enormous detail in the state document, this is fortunate. On the other hand, the large number of amendments that have resulted have only added to the detail.

THE CONTINUING CONTROVERSY

The impact of direct democracy should not be exaggerated. Like those of the federal government and all fifty states, California's form of government is basically that of a republic, that is, a *representative* democracy. In California and other states (mostly west of the Mississippi) influenced by the legacy of the Progressives, representative democracy has been modified, not replaced, by an overlay of direct democracy. Whether this was a good idea remains controversial, especially with regard to the initiative. Although it has not altered the state's basic form of government, the initiative process has certainly had a significant impact.

In the first place, the fact that most constitutional amendments come through referendums rather than initiatives is a little misleading, as is the fact that the vast majority of statutes become law through the normal legislative process. Initiatives often deal with major and controversial issues. In recent decades voters have approved constitutional or statute initiatives that, among other things

- restored the death penalty;
- sharply reduced property taxes and made it harder for local governments to increase taxes, fees, and other charges;
- changed the rules for criminal proceedings in ways designed to strengthen the hand of the prosecution;
- established the California Lottery;
- guaranteed public schools (kindergarten through community colleges) over 40 percent of the state general fund;
- made the insurance commissioner an elected office;
- set term limits for members of the state legislature and elected state executives;
- banned race and gender preferences by state and local government entities in employment, education, and contracting;
- legalized (under state, but not federal, law) the use of marijuana for medical purposes;
- curtailed bilingual education.

Sometimes initiatives have an impact on the political process that is indirect, but still important. The prospect of an initiative campaign can sometimes spur the legislature and governor into action. For example, legislation to expand charter schools became law in 1998 only after supporters had warned that if it did not, they would go to the voters with a more sweeping proposal.[37] A threat to put one initiative on the ballot can also be used to influence the outcome of another. In 1998, organized labor persuaded many businesses to remain neutral on a measure that would have restricted the ability of unions to raise campaign funds—by threatening to launch another measure that would have restricted the political activities of corporations.[38] Initiatives have also been used by office seekers as a device for publicizing their candidacies. In 2002, Arnold Schwarzenegger played a key role in the passage of Proposition 49, which provides state grants for before and after school programs. This was widely viewed as an attempt to establish his political credibility for a run for governor in 2006. The 2003 recall of Governor Davis provided Schwarzenegger with an earlier than expected opportunity to achieve this goal. Since becoming governor, Schwarzenegger has used threats to go to the people on a number of issues (such as workers' compensation reform) as a tool in negotiations with the legislature and with various interest groups.

The initiative process has been sharply criticized on several grounds. One newspaper editorial has called it "the monster that threatens California politics."[39]

Critics argue that initiatives are often extremely complicated, and that to expect voters to make informed decisions about them involves unrealistic assumptions about the amount of time a voter can be expected to spend studying the ballot. In one poll, respondents estimated that they would spend on average about two hours reading the ballot pamphlet distributed by the secretary of state for an election that was to take place the next month.[40] Even if we take this optimistic figure at face value, this worked out to about thirty seconds per page of very small print. Moreover, by its nature, the initiative process requires voters to consider proposals on a piecemeal basis despite the complex interconnection of public policies.

Critics also contend that, instead of giving "power to the people," the process gives power to well-financed interests. One writer argues that the initiative process "has become the favored tool of millionaires and interest groups that use their wealth to achieve their own policy goals."[41] The spending record (so far) was set in 1998, when a total of $66 million was expended, mostly by Native American tribes, in a successful campaign for Proposition 5, permitting Nevada-style tribal casinos. Opponents, mostly Nevada casinos, spent $26 million in a losing cause.[42]

The influence of money on the initiative process may be exaggerated. A study by Elizabeth Gerber found that although expenditure of large sums of money may be effective in defeating an initiative, it is usually not enough to bring about passage. (Her research was, however, completed before passage of the casino initiative.)[43]

Yet another criticism of initiatives is their "take it or leave it" nature. Voters may use them to "send a message" to Sacramento, but they can be very blunt instruments that do not allow for give and take among different interests, and they may not adequately represent those on the losing side.

Controversy over initiatives often continues long after passage, and a number of initiatives have been ruled unconstitutional, in whole or in part, by state or federal courts.[44] Among such measures have been those written to regulate campaign finance, curtail services to illegal immigrants, rewrite the state's insurance laws, and establish a blanket primary. Many initiatives face court challenges simply because of their highly controversial nature. In addition, the fact that initiatives are written by one side means that the losing side has little alternative other than to resort to the courts.[45] Some initiatives are open to challenges because they are poorly drafted: unlike measures that go through the legislature, they do not have to be reviewed by the Office of the Legislative Counsel. Overturning of initiatives by the courts is either, depending on one's view of the particular measure in question or of the initiative process in general, a valuable exercise in checks and balances or an arrogant indifference to the will of the people. Then again, the courts do not always have the last word. After a statute initiative allowing casino gambling on tribal lands was declared unconstitutional by the California Supreme Court in August 1999, voters in March 2000 approved a referendum amending the state constitution to override the court's objection.

Despite criticisms, opinion polls continue to show that, by wide margins, Californians think that ballot propositions are a good thing. In fact, two-thirds of the Californians who were surveyed even favored extension of ballot propositions to national elections.[46] They have, however, expressed unhappiness with some aspects of the process, and support, while still strong, may have declined somewhat from earlier levels.[47]

Direct democracy, in short, seems here to stay. A number of changes to the process, however, have been suggested:[48] These suggestions are intended to serve several different goals:

- The number of initiatives could be reduced by increasing the number of signatures required to put an initiative on the ballot.

- The importance of money could be reduced by outlawing or limiting the use of paid petition circulators. Another way might be to require fuller disclosure of the sources of money spent on campaign ads.

- The burden on the voter might be eased, for example, by making more information about initiative campaigns available electronically.

- "Majority tyranny" might be combatted by requiring a two-thirds vote for passage or by allowing initiatives on the ballot only in general elections (when voter turnout is higher than in primaries).

- The technical and legal quality of initiatives could be improved by requiring that initiatives be reviewed by the legislative counsel, the secretary of state, or some other expert entity.

- The role of representative government could be increased by making it easier for the legislature to amend an initiative or review it before it is placed on the ballot.

(© 2001 Mark Fiore)

SURFING CALIFORNIA: INTERNET RESOURCES

The California Constitution is available online at:

> *http://www.leginfo.ca.gov/const.html*

It can be examined either by keyword searches or by clicking on "Table of Contents," then on the particular article you wish to examine. Try going to Article 1, the "Declaration of Rights." Compare what you find there to the Bill of Rights (the first ten amendments) of the U.S. Constitution. Browse some of the other articles to see just how detailed the state constitution is.

Other sites related to this chapter include:

A bibliography of books, articles, and Internet sites dealing with the initiative process in California:

> *http://www.igs.berkeley.edu/library/bibliog/initiative.html*

Summaries of all statewide measures placed on the ballot under the current constitution:

> *http://lalaw.lib.ca.us/ballot.html*

A searchable database of ballot propositions:

> *http://library.uchastings.edu/library/Research%20Databases/CA%20Ballot%20Measures/ca_ballot_measures_main.htm*

A comprehensive source of information about recalls:

> *http://www.igs.berkeley.edu/library/htRecall2003.html*

3. Public Opinion and the Media

A political rally in California consists of three people around a television set.
—ROBERT SHRUM[1]

California is more like the rest of the country than it is different. This certainly applies to patterns of public opinion and to the ways in which people acquire such opinions. The family plays a key role in early political socialization. Religious, educational, economic, and other institutions also influence how people think about politics in general and influence their views on specific issues. Most of the things that help explain differences of opinion (such as social class, gender, and religious affiliation) probably operate in California in at least roughly the same ways that they do in other states. There are, however, a few questions that deserve special attention in the California context. In this chapter, we will look at whether there are major regional differences in public opinion within California. Because of California's vast and growing ethnic diversity, we will analyze the opinions of the state's different ethnic groups. Finally, because the mass media are especially important in a state with a population as mobile as California's, we will examine the role that is played by the media as conduits and gatekeepers of politically relevant information.

HOW PEOPLE THINK ABOUT POLITICS

It is customary to classify people as either liberal (sometimes called "left") or conservative (or "right") on political issues. Doing so obviously oversimplifies matters considerably, because most people take liberal positions on some issues and conservative positions on others. Some sort of shorthand, nevertheless, is needed to describe people's political philosophies.

Almost everyone would agree that freedom, order, and equality are all good things. By its nature, law places limits on human freedom, and so dilemmas are created when laws constrain freedom to attain other desirable goals. Kenneth Janda, Jeffrey M. Berry, and

Jerry Goldman[2] suggest that we can sort out different ideologies (related sets of political beliefs) by the ways in which these dilemmas are resolved. Historically, the original dilemma involved trade-offs between freedom and order. A modern dilemma has arisen over trade-offs between freedom and equality. Many current political controversies can be understood in terms of one or the other of these dilemmas.

On the one hand, **liberals** are more likely to oppose laws that limit freedom in order to maintain order while **conservatives** tend to favor such laws. On the other hand, liberals are more willing to use the law to limit freedom in order to promote equality while conservatives tend to resist these efforts. Those who resolve both dilemmas in favor of less government (that is, who favor freedom over both order and equality) are usually called **libertarians** because their highest political value is freedom (or liberty). Janda and his colleagues refer to the libertarians' opposites, those who emphasize both order and equality over freedom, as **communitarians** because they emphasize the values of the community and the value of community itself. Figure 3.1 summarizes these four ideological types and provides examples of the sorts of issue positions each embraces.

Obviously, not all political controversies can be categorized in this fashion. Gun control is an example. On this issue *liberals,* to maintain order, support laws regulating firearms.

FIGURE 3.1
Political Ideologies

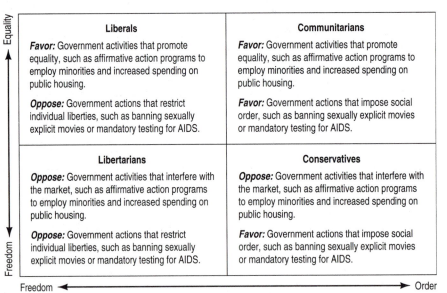

SOURCE: Kenneth Janda, Jeffrey M. Berry, and Jerry Goldman, *The Challenge of Democracy,* Eighth Edition. Copyright © 2005 by Houghton Mifflin Company. Reprinted with permission.

IS CALIFORNIA DIFFERENT?

University of California, Berkeley sociologist Michael Hout has compared political opinions of Californians with those of other Americans. His data, taken from surveys conducted in the 1990s, show that Californians tend to be more liberal on both economic and social issues. Economically, Californians were more likely to favor increasing government spending for a variety of domestic programs. Socially, Californians held more liberal views regarding abortion, homosexuality, and legalization of marijuana and suicide.[3]

REGIONS

In the June 1992 primary, voters in thirty-one northern California counties cast ballots on advisory (nonbinding) measures asking whether California should be divided into two separate states. The measure to separate passed in all but four counties. Although these votes were merely advisory, the outcome suggested renewed interest in an idea that has been pursued, with varying degrees of interest, ever since California's earliest days as a state.

Differences between northern and southern California have long been regarded by some observers as a factor of considerable importance in the state's politics.[4] Sometimes, such differences have been described in terms that are unusually colorful for academic discourse. Two northern California scholars, in a book about the state's political history, once described "the trepidations civilized Californians have felt toward the southern part of the state."[5] While the rhetoric is usually more toned down, perceptions of strong north-south differences in the state persist, with the south described as the more conservative region.

The reality is rather different. If there is any overall regional pattern in California's politics, it is less a north-south split than a division between the coast and the interior. Generally speaking (but with notable exceptions), as one travels from west to east in California, one also moves from left to right politically. This pattern can be seen fairly clearly in Map 3.1, which shows the winner of the 2004 presidential race in each county. With a few exceptions, counties bordering on the Pacific Ocean went for Democrat John Kerry, while most inland counties gave more votes to Republican George W. Bush. The division between Republican and Democratic counties has been quite stable in recent years. In 2003, Gray Davis lost the recall election statewide by about the same margin by which Democrat Al Gore had won the state three years earlier. Despite this, only five counties (Imperial, Lake, Sacramento, San Benito, and Santa Barbara) that had supported Gore voted against Davis, while all counties that had voted for Bush opted for the recall. Only two counties, Alpine and Mono, voted for a different party's presidential candidate in 2004 than they had four years earlier. Initial 2004 returns in Mono County showed Kerry and Bush tied at 2,200 votes each, but a recount gave the edge to Kerry by 7 votes.[6]

Don't look for a partitioning of California any time soon. All the counties in which voters in 1992 approved ballot measures to divide California were sparsely populated, and no serious effort has been made to pursue the matter further.[7] A Field Poll in November 1993 showed that, statewide, respondents rejected the idea of dividing the state by a two-to-one margin.[8] Even more important, splitting the state would require approval by the U.S. Congress. If California were to become two separate states it would be entitled to four seats in the U.S. Senate instead of two. This is not an idea that senators from the other states are likely to endorse.

MAP 3.1
California's Political Geography: 2004 Presidential Election

ETHNICITY

Table 3.1 describes the voting of the state's four major ethnic groups on twenty statewide propositions on the ballot from November 1994 through November 2004, as measured by exit polls conducted by the *Los Angeles Times*. The propositions included are those for which exit polls conducted by the *Times* found differences of at least 20 percentage points in the voting of self-identified liberals and conservatives, and for which the results were broken down by the ethnic groups shown in the table. Numbers compare the percentage in each group casting "liberal" votes, with positive numbers indicating that the group was more liberal than voters as a whole, and negative numbers indicating a more conservative voting pattern.[9]

On most issues, Anglos are most conservative in their voting, with African Americans and Latinos most liberal, and Asian Americans somewhere in between. (The principal

TABLE 3.1
Voting on Statewide Propositions by Ethnicity: Percent More (Less) Liberal Than All Respondents

Topic	Prop.	Date	Anglo	Latino	African American	Asian American
Illegal Immigration	187	Nov. 1994	−5	35	11	11
Affirmative Action	209	Nov. 1996	−9	30	28	15
Medical Marijuana	215	Nov. 1996	0	−7	14	−7
Health Care	216	Nov. 1996	−3	4	9	7
Union Dues	226	June 1998	−7	23	17	0
Bilingual Education	227	June 1998	−6	24	13	4
Tribal Gaming	5	Nov. 1998	−5	11	16	2
Gay Marriage	22	Mar. 2000	1	−6	−3	0
Tribal Gaming	1A	Mar. 2000	−3	10	19	−7
School Bonds	26	Mar. 2000	−1	12	13	−3
School Vouchers	38	Nov. 2000	−1	6	−3	−5
School Bonds	38	Nov. 2000	−2	8	8	5
Clean Water Bond	40	Mar. 2002	−3	16	19	2
Term Limits	45	Mar. 2002	−2	14	16	3
Same Day Registration	52	Nov. 2002	−5	11	25	13
Racial Classifications	54	Oct. 2003	−2	11	23	8
School Bonds	55	Mar. 2004	−3	14	17	4
Taxation	56	Mar. 2004	−1	8	7	1
Embryonic Stem Cells	71	Nov. 2004	−4	1	8	12
Health Insurance	72	Nov. 2004	−7	15	26	10
Average			−3	12	14	4

NOTE: Measures of statistical significance were not provided, and numbers of cases for the non-Anglo groups were relatively small.

SOURCE: Derived from data in *Los Angeles Times Poll, http://www.latimes.com/news/custom/timespoll/.*

reason why the votes of Anglos differ relatively little from the overall vote is that, as will be discussed in Chapter 5, Anglos constitute a much larger proportion of voters than of the total population. In the *Times* exit polls, they made up 64 to 84 percent of the vote, and so are heavily reflected in the overall totals.)

Not all results conformed to this general pattern. Some social issues produced unique configurations. On Proposition 215, decriminalizing use of marijuana for medicinal purposes, Latinos and Asian Americans were most conservative while Latinos and African Americans were a little more conservative than other voters on gay marriage. Asian Americans and African Americans were a little more conservative than other voters on the question of school vouchers.

Measures dealing specifically with ethnic issues did tend to polarize voters along ethnic lines. Proposition 187 (curtailing services for illegal immigrants) and Proposition 227 (curbing bilingual education) produced large gaps between Latinos and Anglos, with African Americans and Asian Americans in between. Proposition 209 (banning race and gender preferences in state programs) also received strong support from Anglos; Latinos and African Americans were most strongly opposed.

In short, the relationship between ethnicity and ideology is complicated. This is even more true when important differences within groups are taken into account. A study in the 1980s by Bruce Cain and Roderick Kiewiet showed, for example, that Japanese Americans were more likely than other Asian Americans to hold views similar to those of most Anglos.[10] Also (though not shown in Table 3.1), about a third of Anglos voted to continue bilingual education programs while almost as large a proportion of Latinos voted to curtail them. These complex patterns may be frustrating for leaders trying to form ethnically based political coalitions. On the other hand, they probably tend to lessen the severity of ethnic conflict. Your adversary on one issue may be your ally on another. These exceptions to the rule should serve, in addition, as a caution against pigeonholing people based on their ethnicity. Ethnicity is only one of a number of "explanatory variables" that need to be taken into account in understanding political attitudes.

THE MEDIA

Media coverage of California politics presents something of a paradox. In some ways, it is quite extensive. As Thad Beyle writes, "California is clearly the leader in media markets because there are so many large communities to be served in the state."[11] Races for governor, and sometimes other offices, are the focus of attention throughout the country as are California's controversial ballot initiatives. As the quote that opened this chapter suggests, political campaigns in California, except in local elections outside large cities, are predominantly "air wars" rather than "ground wars," with millions of dollars spent for paid ads on radio and, especially, on television to support or oppose candidates and ballot propositions. Unpaid (and arguably more objective) media coverage of campaigns, however, focuses disproportionately on races for president or governor, and on a few hot button propositions. Contests for other offices and over most propositions receive far less attention.[12] Even for the most heavily covered campaigns, voters often get much more information about the horse race aspects of the contests (that is, which side is ahead or behind and what strategies it is pursuing) than substantive information about issues and candidates.

When it comes to the day-to-day operations of state government, media attention may be even more superficial. As one critic described coverage of the state legislature, "[c]ommercial stations will cover the state Assembly and Senate . . . only when Democrats and Republicans start chasing each other in cars on freeways. Equating Sacramento with Jupiter and Uranus, they're waiting for a spaceship to get them there."[13] A study sponsored by the Center for Responsive Government analyzed the amount of coverage of state government by leading broadcast and print media.[14] The study focused on a two-week period in late summer when activity in the state legislature was at its peak. The researchers found that during a typical television news hour, 2.9 percent of the time, or about 1 minute and 44 seconds, was devoted to state government. The figures for all-news radio stations was about the same: 3.2 percent, or about 1 minute and 55 seconds. Newspapers did somewhat better, devoting an average of 171 column inches of text each day to state government.

This lack of coverage is partly a function of the fact that there is nothing in Sacramento comparable to the large Washington press corps that covers the federal government. Following the election of Arnold Schwarzenegger, television stations in Los Angeles and San Francisco reopened Sacramento bureaus that had been closed for a number of years.[15] Whether these bureaus will outlast the tenure of a celebrity governor remains to be seen. Newspapers again provide somewhat more extensive coverage; a 2003 survey by the Project on the State of the American Newspaper found a total of 40 full-time reporters covering government in the state capital for a dozen daily papers and three consortiums serving another 16 papers. The largest bureaus were those of the *Sacramento Bee* (with ten full-time reporters) and the *Los Angeles Times* (with six).[16]

In recent years, the United States Congress has televised its proceedings over C-SPAN (Cable–Satellite Public Affairs Network) in an attempt to overcome the relative lack of attention paid it by the media. For similar reasons, the proceedings of the state legislature are televised over the California Channel. Unlike the C-SPAN networks, however, the California Channel does not provide gavel-to-gavel coverage of floor proceedings, is not on the air around the clock, and is available in fewer markets.

Cable services also televise meetings of city councils and other local governments. For the most part, however, local news coverage tends to be focused on the sensational. You are more likely to see a car chase or a warehouse fire on the evening news than a story about what is going on in local government. Local newspapers and radio and television stations provide little information about the routine, but important activities of counties, cities, and special districts. The enormous complexity of local government also helps explain the superficiality of media coverage. This is especially true for special purpose governments (with the partial exception of school districts, which generally receive much more coverage than other special districts). Though these local governments sometimes exercise great power, they often labor in near anonymity. Their arcane structures and jurisdictions make it inherently difficult for the media to help make them accountable to the public by publicizing and analyzing their work.

A Field Poll survey found that Californians are generally uninterested in government and politics.[17] It is an open question whether this is a cause or an effect of the relative inattentiveness of the media to these subjects.

SURFING CALIFORNIA: INTERNET RESOURCES

Janda, Berry, and Goldman have developed a program, IDEAlog, which you can use to see how you fit into the ideological classification described in this chapter. To take their test, go to *http://idealog.org/*.

Advocates for Self-Government offers "The World's Shortest Political Quiz," at *http://www.self-gov.org/wspq.html*. Take the quiz. Your views will be classified using a scheme similar to that found in this chapter, except that what we've called "communitarian" is called "statist" and there is an additional "centrist" category. Note that Advocates for Self-Government is unabashedly libertarian. Their terminology (like "self-government" and "statist") clearly reflects this perspective.

At present, hundreds of California newspapers and radio stations are available on-line. Comprehensive lists for the state (and the whole world!) are provided by:

American Journalism Review NewsLink:

http://newslink.org/

NewsVoyager:

http://www.newspaperlinks.com/voyager.cfm

Radio-locator:

http://www.radio-locator.com/

Sites for some of the state's top newspapers are:

Los Angeles Times: http://www.latimes.com (free registration required)

Orange County Register: http://www.ocregister.com (free registration required)

Sacramento Bee: http://www.sacbee.com

San Diego Union-Tribune: http://www.uniontribune.com

San Jose Mercury News: http://www.mercurynews.com/mld/mercurynews/ (free registration required)

San Francisco Chronicle: http://www.sfgate.com/chronicle

Rough & Tumble: A Daily Snapshot of California Public Policy and Politics offers full text of current news articles, from various sources, with a focus on California politics and policies at *http://www.rtumble.com*.

Sacramento Bee columnist Daniel Weintraub authors a Weblog on California called the California Insider at *http://www.sacbee.com/static/weblogs/insider/*.

4. Political Parties and Interest Groups

This is my dilemma: If I had stayed away from the lobbyists, I would have been ineffective. If I take their money and do nothing for it, I am a cheat. If I do their bidding, I could be cheating the public. I find myself rationalizing what I have done. The tragedy is that I may wind up serving the very elements I set out to beat—yet not know that I have changed.

—JESSE UNRUH[1]

$\mathcal{P}$ olitical parties and interest groups are often seen, sometimes with justification, as exerting a corrupting influence on politics. Parties are routinely described as "machines," led by "bosses," while interest groups (and the lobbyists who represent them) are vilified as "pressure groups" or "special interests." However, both parties and interest groups have essential roles to play in organizing people's opinions and interests and bringing these to bear on governmental decisions.

PARTIES

One author has written that "the key element of California's political style is anti-partyism."[2] An article in the *California Journal,* however, stated that "in the California legislature, Democrats are almost exclusively liberal and Republicans nearly all conservative,"[3] suggesting that the spirit of the party system is alive and well in the state.

Each of these seemingly contradictory statements is perfectly true. Political party organizations in California traditionally have been weak and in many ways remain so. It is equally correct, however, to say that California Republicans and California Democrats think and behave very differently. This is true of those who vote in party primaries. It is even more true of those who hold elected office.

Following a distinction made by political scientist Frank Sorauf, we will discuss separately (1) the official party organization, (2) the party in the electorate, and (3) the party in government.[4] Party organizations will be the focus of this chapter. The party in the electorate and in government will be touched on here and examined in greater detail in subsequent chapters.

Almost a century ago, the **Progressives** set out to weaken California's political parties, and to a considerable degree succeeded.[5] In Chapter 2, we saw how the initiative process has worked to undercut both parties and the state legislature. In this chapter and in Chapter 5, we will examine the **primary** as a mechanism that takes away from party organizations control over their own nominations. This, too, is a product of the Progressive Era. In this chapter, we will also show how the internal operations of party organizations have been limited. In Chapter 5, we will show how in California, unlike a number of other states, local and judicial offices are chosen on a nonpartisan basis. In Chapter 9, we will explain how in most California cities and counties, the day-to-day administration of government is run by professional managers rather than by elected politicians.

Party Organizations and Primary Elections

Before running in the November general election, candidates must first survive a primary election in the spring. Since their invention in California and other states heavily influenced by the Progressives, primaries have by now spread throughout the country, but they play a much more limited role in some states. Some have mixed primary/convention systems. In Iowa, for example, if no candidate for an office receives at least 35 percent of the votes in the primary, the nomination is made by party delegates at the party's convention. In Indiana, primaries are held only for some offices, while nominations for others are made at conventions.[6] In states like California, on the other hand, the voters pick all nominees, with the party organization having no direct say in the outcome.

For a number of years, California parties were prohibited from endorsing candidates in their own primaries. Some party activists filed suit against this restriction, challenging it as a violation of their constitutional rights to freedom of expression. In 1989, the U.S. Supreme Court agreed with them and lifted the prohibition. The same decision also granted parties authority to determine their own organizational structures, which, until then, had been specified in detail in state law.[7] Later court rulings also overturned a measure approved by voters in 1986 prohibiting parties from endorsing candidates in nonpartisan elections.[8]

The right of political parties to make endorsements has so far made little difference. In some states with traditions of strong party organizations, such endorsements carry great weight with voters. In 1990 the California Democratic Party endorsed John Van de Camp as its nominee for governor, but he lost the primary to Dianne Feinstein.[9] In 1994 and 1998, the Democratic Party decided not to endorse any candidate for governor, fearing that to do so would be too divisive.[10] If party organizations were strong, an endorsement would be a way to *overcome* divisiveness.

A bigger change affecting the role of parties in California was the adoption by voters in 1996 of Proposition 198, which was designed to weaken parties further as organizations. Proposition 198 provided for a **blanket primary,** a method that was also in use in Alaska and Washington. For each office, candidates of all parties were listed in random order, and a voter, regardless of his or her party registration, could choose any candidate. The candidate of each party receiving the most votes became that party's nominee. Prior to adoption of Proposition 198, California had a **closed primary.** Voters who were registered with a party were restricted to choosing from among that party's candidates in the primary, while independents (who register as "decline to state") were unable to vote in partisan primaries at all. Under the new system adopted in 1996, voters could (except in elections to choose local party committee members) freely "cross over" to vote for candidates of any party for any given office. The blanket primary first went into effect in 1998 and continued through the March 7 primaries in 2000.

California's party organizations strongly opposed the new system, objecting to participation in their primaries by voters loyal to other parties or to none. The Democratic, Republican, Libertarian, and Peace and Freedom parties joined in suing to have Proposition 198 declared unconstitutional. Each feared that one party might be tempted to raid another party's primary by encouraging its own supporters to vote for the weakest opposition candidate. Supporters of the blanket primary hoped that the new system would make it easier for moderates to win nomination by appealing beyond the relatively narrow constituencies of their own parties to voters registered with other parties or as independents.

The 2000 primaries provided some evidence for this latter notion. The California secretary of state provided a breakdown of results by all voters and by party registration. In most cases, the outcome was unaffected. In the presidential primaries, for example, George W. Bush and Al Gore won their parties' primaries regardless of whether crossover voters were included in the tabulation. In three Republican assembly races, however, the more conservative contestant won among Republican voters, but cross-over votes provided the margin of victory for more middle-of-the-road opponents.

In June 2000, the U.S. Supreme Court, by a margin of 7 to 2, sided with the parties, holding that the blanket primary violated a party's right under the federal constitution to freedom of association. On behalf of the majority, Justice Antonin Scalia wrote that "Proposition 198 forces political parties to associate with—to have their nominees, and hence their positions, determined by—those who, at best, have refused to affiliate with the party, and, at worst, have expressly affiliated with a rival."[11]

Recognizing the popularity of the blanket primary, the state legislature then passed legislation allowing, but not requiring, parties to permit decline-to-state registrants to vote in their primaries. Both the Republican and Democratic parties opted to do so, though Republican Party rules did not allow non-Republican voters to participate in presidential primaries, and neither party allowed nonmembers to vote in elections for the parties' county central committees.

In his opinion invalidating Proposition 198, Scalia suggested that an alternative to the blanket primary, usually called the **open primary**,[12] might be constitutional. In this system, voters may, on election day, choose any party's primary ballot, but must vote in that party's primary contests for all offices and may not "mix and match" by voting for any candidate they wish in each contest.

Another idea that Scalia suggested might pass constitutional muster became the basis for Proposition 62 on the November 2004 ballot. This initiative would have, in effect, created a nonpartisan primary. Except in presidential elections and in contests for party central committees, all candidates would have run on the same primary ballot. The top two finishers, even if both were from the same party, would then have faced each other in the general election. The measure was defeated.

Party Organizations: Structures and Activities

Even the internal structures of California parties are weak. The basic organizational unit of the California Republican Party is the County Central Committee, selected by registered Republican voters in the party primary.[13] The California Democratic Party's organization is similar except that at the local level there are, in addition to the County Central Committees, committees within each assembly district.[14] In neither party are there grass roots precinct organizations, such as are found in some states with stronger parties.

Neither the local party organizations nor their state central committees are in a position to give direction to members of the party who hold public office. The latter are free to ignore positions taken in the party platform. The parties' activities and pronouncements generally receive little attention in the media. Republican chair George Sundheim enjoys very little name recognition. Democratic chair Art Torres is better known, but this is in large part due to his record as a former state legislator and past candidate for insurance commissioner.

Party organizations in California have little patronage at their disposal.[15] California has a very extensive civil service system through which almost all jobs with the state government are awarded. Instead of serving as rewards for party loyalists, civil service jobs are obtained through examinations or other competitive processes.

One very key area in which parties do play a significant role is fund raising. The impact on parties of recent changes at both the federal and state level in regulation of campaign finance is still unfolding. Proposition 34, passed in 2000, provides for much higher and looser limits on campaign contributions when made through political parties.[16] As a result, party committees are commanding increasing respect and influence.[17]

On the other hand, a new law passed at the federal level in 2002 may have the opposite effect. In recent years, federal law had strengthened party organizations in California and elsewhere by encouraging contributions to state parties of "soft money" (ostensibly used for "party building activities" such as voter registration drives). The new McCain-Feingold campaign reform act, however, imposes new restrictions on soft money that, while aimed at federal elections, may spill over into state and local contests and limit the role played by party organizations.[18]

The Party in the Electorate

The parties nevertheless are critically important to an understanding of the state's politics. The two major parties have represented very distinctive coalitions of voters. Differences between Democratic and Republican voters have been especially clear and especially important in primary elections. As evidenced by low voter turnout, only the more politically committed participate in primaries. Because primary elections determine who the parties' nominees will be, these voters virtually decide what sort of Republicans and Democrats will go to Sacramento and Washington, D.C.

Table 4.1 describes registered voters surveyed by The Field Institute in February 2003. Among Republicans, self-described conservatives outnumbered liberals seventeen to one. Among Democrats, on the other hand, those who called themselves liberal outnumbered those who called themselves conservatives by about two and a half to one.

There are also clear differences of attitude on specific issues. Table 4.2 compares the responses of Republicans and Democrats in exit polls by the *Los Angeles Times* asking respondents how they had voted on various statewide propositions in recent years.[19] In each case, Republicans were more conservative in their voting behavior. On all measures, differences between the parties were clear. Majorities of Democrats cast liberal votes in twenty of the twenty-two measures included in the table, while majorities of Republicans were conservative with equal consistency. Ironically the primary, which the Progressives set up in a successful effort to weaken parties as organizations has actually served, at least in recent years, to make party differences in the electorate more important and to force each of the two major parties to respond to a very different base of core constituents.

Differences between ordinary Republican and Democratic voters are magnified among activists who attend rallies, contribute money, and help get out the vote. Such activists tend to be more consistently ideological than ordinary citizens: more liberal if they are Democrats, more conservative if Republicans. As a consequence, they tend to pull the parties even further apart.

The Party in Government

Not surprisingly, the liberal-dominated electorate voting in Democratic primaries has usually chosen liberals as party nominees. The opposite is the case in conservative-dominated Republican primaries. The result is that it is very difficult for a liberal to win a Republican primary or for a conservative to win a primary on the Democratic side. Even during California's brief experiment with the blanket primary, exceptions to this rule remained uncommon. The implications of this ideological polarization between the parties will be spelled out in greater detail in Chapter 6.

TABLE 4.1

Self-Described Ideology, Percent by Party Registration

	Republicans	Democrats
Conservative	68	16
Middle of the Road	28	45
Liberal	4	39
Total	100	100

SOURCE: Analysis by author of February 2003 Field Poll.

TABLE 4.2

Voting on Statewide Propositions by Party—Percent Liberal

Topic	Prop.	Date	Democrats	Republicans	Difference
Illegal Immigration	187	Nov. 1994	64	22	42
Contingency Fees	201	Nov. 1996	70	44	26
Contingency Fees	202	Nov. 1996	64	39	25
Affirmative Action	209	Nov. 1996	69	20	49
Medical Marijuana	215	Nov. 1996	70	34	36
Health Care	216	Nov. 1996	49	21	28
Union Dues	226	June 1998	72	28	44
Bilingual Education	227	June 1998	53	23	30
Tribal Gaming	5	Nov. 1998	75	46	29
Gay Marriage	22	Mar. 2000	57	20	37
Tribal Gaming	1A	Mar. 2000	72	54	18
School Bonds	26	Mar. 2000	67	30	37
School Vouchers	38	Nov. 2000	83	53	30
School Bonds	38	Nov. 2000	66	35	31
Clean Water Bond	40	Mar. 2002	77	33	44
Term Limits	45	Mar. 2002	58	26	32
Same Day Registration	52	Nov. 2002	54	23	31
Racial Classifications	54	Oct. 2003	82	45	37
School Bonds	55	Mar. 2004	63	34	29
Taxation	56	Mar. 2004	47	19	28
Embryonic Stem Cells	71	Nov. 2004	77	37	40
Health Insurance	72	Nov. 2004	72	21	51
Average					34

NOTE: Measures of statistical significance were not provided. The *Times* variously refers to respondents' "party registration," "party affiliation," or "party self-identification."

SOURCE: Derived from data in *Los Angeles Times Poll, http://www.latimes.com/news/custom/timespoll/.*

Minor Parties

In addition to the Democratic Party and the Republican Party, five minor parties are currently qualified for the ballot.[20]

- **American Independent Party.** The American Independent Party was established in 1967 as part of George Wallace's presidential bid. It is conservative on both social and economic issues.

- **Peace and Freedom Party.** Founded the same year as the American Independent Party, the Peace and Freedom Party grew out of the "New Left" antiwar and civil-rights movements of the 1960s. It is liberal on both social and economic issues. After the 1998 election, the party lost its place on the ballot after falling below the minimum requirement that it receive at least 2 percent of the vote in at least one statewide election. In 2003, it was able to obtain enough registered voters to requalify.

- **Libertarian Party.** Founded in 1971, the Libertarian Party, as its name implies, generally seeks to minimize levels of government programs and believes government activities should be kept to a minimum. This party thus tends to side with conservatives on economic issues and with liberals on most social issues, gun control being a notable exception.

- **Green Party.** The Greens, who qualified for the ballot in 1992, are patterned after parties of the same name that have been founded in Germany and elsewhere. It is liberal on both social and economic issues.

- **Natural Law Party.** Qualifying for the California ballot in 1995, the Natural Law Party was founded by followers of the Maharishi Mahesh Yogi, former spiritual advisor to the Beatles. The party contends that "government can solve problems at their bases through scientifically proven programs to bring every citizen, and the entire nation, into accord with natural law."

Another party, the **Reform Party,** originally founded by Ross Perot, was on the ballot until recently. The party has, to say the least, been inconsistent in liberal-conservative terms. In 2000, the conservative and libertarian wings of the party became deeply divided at its national convention over its presidential nominee. Conservative Pat Buchanan prevailed over John Hagelin, who went on to run as the nominee of the Natural Law Party. Four years later, liberal Ralph Nader, who had run as the Green Party candidate for president in 2000, won the endorsement of the Reform Party at the national level. By then, however, the party had lost its place on the California ballot after the 2002 elections and, as of this writing, is seeking to obtain enough voter registrations to requalify. Together, the minor parties currently on the ballot have won a partisan election only once. This occurred in March 1999 when Green Party candidate Audie Bock won a special election to fill a vacant seat in the state assembly. The Greens' jubilation was short-lived. Some months later, Bock switched her affiliation to independent. In 2000, she was defeated by Democrat Wilma Chan.

This does not mean that minor parties are irrelevant. Members of such parties have won some local offices in officially nonpartisan contests. In San Francisco in 2003, Green Party candidate Matt Gonzalez almost upset Democrat Gavin Newsom in the race for mayor. Moreover, by staking out clearly defined positions on issues, minor parties can provide a counterweight to the tendency of the Democrats and Republicans to move toward the center in search of votes. From the point of view of the minor parties, they serve to keep the major parties honest. This is, however, a two-edged sword, because in a close election there is a danger that a minor party will take votes away from the party that it might well consider to be the lesser of two evils. For this reason, the addition of the Green Party to the ballot was of greater concern to Democrats than to Republicans (and, at the national level, played an important role in the 2000 presidential election). In any case, as a practical matter the real impact of minor parties is not to win elections, but to exert influence on those who do. In other words, though structured as parties, they actually function more like interest groups.

INTEREST GROUPS

As we saw in Chapter 2, the railroads were once California's dominant interest group. Later, because of political setbacks and technological change, their influence declined. The state continued to be one in which interest groups were strong, but now a number of different groups had to contend for a share of power.

To assist these groups, the profession of lobbyists developed to serve as brokers between interests and elected officials. The most notorious of these was Artie Samish, whose powers in the 1930s and 1940s rivaled those of the governor. Samish was able to use the money he collected from the groups he represented to "select and elect" cooperative legislators. He was eventually exposed in a 1949 magazine article.[21] The accompanying cover photo of that magazine shows "the secret boss of California" posing with a dummy called "Mr. Legislator." Not surprisingly, legislators did not react positively. Eventually sent to prison for evasion of taxes, Samish later wrote his autobiography, titling it *The Secret Boss of California*.[22]

Today, California remains a state in which various interest groups remain strong.[23] The range of these groups is very broad. Not all important interest groups are fat cats. Numerous grass-roots organizations have played increasingly important roles. These groups are not easily categorized. They vary in terms of philosophy (representing, for example, both sides of debates over issues such as abortion), motivation (some brought together by deeply held convictions; others by self-interest, enlightened or otherwise), and breadth of concerns (single or multiple issues).

Despite the fact that interest-group activity is essential to democracy (and protected by the U.S. Bill of Rights' guarantee of freedom to "petition the government for redress of grievances"), lobbyists (those who seek to influence the actions of the legislature or executive agencies) have a serious image problem. This is only partly due to overtly illegal activities. By the standards found in some other states, California politics has been relatively "clean" through the years, though it has not been without its scandals involving interest group advocates. A more basic problem is that, even when groups act within the law, democracy is undermined when "one dollar, one vote" replaces "one person, one vote."

In the 2001–2002 session of the state legislature, over $390 million was spent on lobbying.[24] Table 4.3 lists the twenty top contributors. Not surprisingly, most had an obvious interest in policies made in the state capital, including businesses (especially those that are heavily regulated by the state, such as utilities), public employee unions, and local governments.

Most groups with a stake in influencing state policy rely on professional lobbying firms, which know their way around the halls of government. Leading the list in 2001–2002 was the firm of Kahl/Pownall Advocates, receiving over $9 million from a total of forty-nine clients. Sixty-seven other firms also received payments of over $1 million for 2001–2002.

Although there may not be anyone around today quite like Artie Samish, Sacramento continues to have its share of powerful and colorful "legislative advocates." One such is Richie Ross, who works both as a lobbyist and as a campaign consultant and who has been

The publication in 1949 of this photo of legendary lobbyist Artie Samish and "Mr. Legislature" helped lead to Samish's downfall. *(Courtesy of the Boston Public Library, Print Department)*

TABLE 4.3

Top 20 Employers of Lobbyists, 2001–2002

Rank	Name	Lobbying Expenditures
1	Edison International & Subsidiaries	$9,633,348
2	California Teachers Association	$6,101,271
3	Western States Petroleum Association	$5,560,104
4	Pacific Telesis Group & Affiliates	$5,159,038
5	California Chamber of Commerce	$4,504,399
6	Pacific Gas and Electric Company	$2,971,492
7	League of California Cities	$2,876,499
8	California Medical Association	$2,541,527
9	Consumer Attorneys of California	$2,522,431
10	BP (British Petroleum) America & Affiliates	$2,469,750
11	California Healthcare Association *et al.*	$2,469,435
12	California Council of Service Employees	$2,273,876
13	California School Employees Association	$2,245,587
14	California Manufacturers and Technology Association	$2,167,192
15	Los Angeles County	$2,036,025
16	Alliance of Automobile Manufacturers	$1,974,209
17	California Building Industry Association	$1,957,277
18	General Motors Corporation	$1,921,820
19	Sempra Energy & Affiliates	$1,918,395
20	California School Boards Association	$1,867,072

SOURCE: California Secretary of State, "Cal-Access: California Automated Lobbying and Campaign Contribution & Expenditure Search System," *http://dbsearch.ss.ca.gov/.*

described as "one of the most feared men in the state."[25] In 2003, Ross made headlines when he was reported to have engaged in what was described as a "profanity-laced tirade" against the chief of staff of one member of the state assembly, and to have threatened to kill the bills sponsored by another member.[26]

There have been a number of attempts over the years to rein in the power of pressure groups. The attacks against the railroads during the Progressive Era in the early years of the century fall within this tradition. Later, after Artie Samish's downfall, the legislature passed the Collier Act to require lobbyists to register with the state and to report their expenditures. In 1974, voters passed the Political Reform Act, which, among other things, sought to curb the "wining and dining" of public officials by lobbyists and to strengthen reporting and disclosure requirements for lobbyists and their interest-group backers. In 1990, voters approved a referendum (Proposition 112) prohibiting members of the legislature from accepting speaking fees. Such fees had been a way for lobbying groups to avoid the laws against gifts to legislators. Closing this loophole, however, leaves lobbyists with numerous other ways to spend their money.

One recent reform may very well have actually increased the importance of interest groups in state politics. Proposition 140, passed by the voters in 1990, limited the terms of office of elected state officials and also reduced by about 38 percent the amount of money that could be spent for legislative staff and other expenses of operating the state legislature.[27] With a shorter "institutional memory" and fewer of its own people to rely on, the state legislature may now be more dependent upon the information provided by interest groups. On the other hand, high rates of turnover also make it harder for lobbyists to maintain relationships with legislators.[28]

SURFING CALIFORNIA: INTERNET RESOURCES

The best place to go for information on California's political parties and interest groups is the California secretary of state's home page:

> *http://www.ss.ca.gov*

For links to the home pages of all seven political parties qualified for the ballot, go to:

> *http://www.ss.ca.gov/elections/elections_f.htm*

For information on lobbying in Sacramento, go to:

> *http://cal-access.ss.ca.gov*

A growing number of state and local interest groups have set up their own home pages. Links to a number of them can be found by going to:

> *http://www.igs.berkeley.edu/library/gallery-ca.html*—scroll down to "Public Policy."

5. Campaigns and Elections

Citizenship is not a spectator sport.

—Robert D. Putnam[1]

When it comes to voting, Californians have ample opportunity to be more than mere spectators. At the statewide level, both primary and general elections are held every even-numbered year. While some local contests are consolidated with statewide elections, other local contests, especially those for city and school district offices, take place at other times. There are occasional special elections as well, at both the statewide and local levels. When they enter the booth, voters must deal with an often lengthy ballot that includes not only various offices but, because of direct democracy, ballot measures on a wide variety of issues.

PARTISAN VERSUS NONPARTISAN ELECTIONS

In **partisan** elections, the contest takes place among candidates of different political parties. In **nonpartisan** contests, candidates run as individuals, without party labels, although in some cases the party affiliation of a candidate may be well known. Of the thousands of elected federal, state, and local offices in California, over 99 percent are nonpartisan. The nonpartisan contests include those for all elected county, city, school, and special district officials, judges, and the state superintendent of public instruction. However, the offices chosen in partisan races are very important. Elections for federal office are partisan. These include elections for president and vice president (running on a joint ticket) and for members of the U.S. Senate and House of Representatives. Members of the state legislature and state executives, except for the superintendent of public instruction, are also chosen on a partisan basis.

In a regular election for a partisan office, each party chooses its nominee in a primary. The winners of the primary face off in a general election runoff. In both primary and runoff elections for partisan office, the winner is the candidate receiving a plurality (that is, more votes than anyone else). In some nonpartisan races as well, a plurality is all that is necessary for victory. In others, if no one wins a majority (over half), a runoff is held between the top two vote-getters.

STATEWIDE ELECTIONS

The Primary

Elections are held throughout the state in even-numbered years for federal, state, and some local offices. At this time, voters cast ballots for partisan federal and state offices and for the members of the parties' county central committees. Voters also choose among candidates for superintendent of public instruction, for judicial offices, and for some local offices. (Of course, not all of the offices just described are on the ballot in every primary, since some have terms of more than two years.) Statewide referendums and initiatives, and sometimes local measures, also appear on the primary election ballot.

In presidential election years, the primary selects delegates to the national conventions that choose presidential and vice-presidential nominees. The California Republican Party uses a winner-take-all system, with all of the top candidate's slate of delegates winning seats at the Republican National Convention. The national Democratic Party requires that delegates be awarded to candidates in a way that is roughly proportional to the vote in the primary, though the method used does favor the leading vote-getters. In addition, the party reserves some seats for uncommitted "superdelegates" (normally elected and party officials). In 2004, 70 of California's 440 delegates to the Democratic National Convention were reserved for superdelegates.[2] Of the remaining 370 delegates, 78 percent were pledged to John Kerry, who had won 64 percent of the vote in the primary. John Edwards, who had captured 20 percent of the vote, received the remaining 22 percent of pledged delegates.[3]

Until recently, the primary had been held on the first Tuesday after the first Monday in June. In presidential election years, this date came late in the process of selecting delegates for the national conventions, and by this time one candidate usually had wrapped up the party's presidential nomination. In 1996, as a one-time experiment, the California primary was moved up to the fourth Tuesday in March in the hope that doing so would give California a role in selecting presidential candidates proportional to its standing as the most populous state. However, several other states also moved up *their* primaries, and by late March it was clear that Republican Bob Dole would join Democrat Bill Clinton as the major party nominees. In 1998, legislation was enacted that permanently moved the primary up even further, to the first Tuesday in March. When even this date proved to be too early to have much impact on the outcome, the state in 2004 again changed the date. Starting in 2006, the primary will again be held in early June.

The General Election

The statewide **general election** is held on the first Tuesday after the first Monday in November of even-numbered years. Elections for partisan offices are held, as are runoff elections, where needed, in nonpartisan races. In addition, contests take place at this time for some local offices that do not require runoffs. Voters also decide on referendums and initiatives that did not qualify in time for the primary ballot.

Special Elections

On occasion, a statewide **special election** may be called. The most recent was in October 2003. In addition to deciding on the recall of Governor Davis and the naming of his replacement, the election also determined the fate of two proposed constitutional amendments that had qualified in time to be included on the ballot. The governor may also issue a proclamation calling for a statewide special election.[4] The last time this happened was in 1993. The election was called by Governor Pete Wilson to consider a constitutional amendment dealing with sales taxes. The ballot ended up consisting of six proposed constitutional amendments and a bond measure.

OTHER LOCAL ELECTIONS

In a number of jurisdictions, local elections are held separately from the statewide contests. Many cities, for example, hold their elections in April of even-numbered years, while many school districts hold theirs in November of odd-numbered years. Special elections can also be held at the local level to fill vacancies (including those in the state legislature and the U.S. House of Representatives), to vote on ballot measures, and to recall office holders.

REGISTRATION

To become a registered voter, one must be a U.S. citizen and California resident who will be at least eighteen years of age by election day. Those in prison or on parole for felonies are ineligible to register, but, unlike some states, California automatically restores the voting rights of felons who have done their time. Also ineligible are those a court has declared mentally incompetent to vote. To register, one simply fills out and sends in a one-page registration form available at, for example, post offices. In addition, voter registration drives often are conducted by parties and interest groups. One can even download a registration form from the secretary of state's Web site.[5] The United States Congress

Church fiesta offers voter registration forms as well as Ferris wheel rides. *(© 2004 Althea Edwards)*

in 1993 passed the "motor-voter" law. As a result of this measure, it is now possible to register at the Department of Motor Vehicles and various other government offices. The voter registration deadline has become progressively more lenient, moving from 54 days before an election to 30 days in 1972, to 29 days in 1975, and to 15 days in 2000. A 2002 initiative to permit same-day registration, however, went down to defeat. Voters must reregister if they change their names or move.

THE BALLOT

California, in common with some but not all other states, uses the **office-bloc ballot**. Ballots in this form list all candidates for a particular office in random order. Like other aspects of California politics discussed in Chapter 4, the office-bloc ballot is intended, at least in a small way, to weaken party organizations. A voter wishing to cast a straight party ballot must hunt around for the candidates of the party of his or her choice. Some states employ a **party-column ballot,** in which all the party's candidates are listed down a column (or across a row). This not only makes it easier for a voter to vote a straight ticket but also makes it easier for a party to organize a campaign around a partisan theme ("Vote Row A All the Way!").

Statewide Propositions were given official numbers beginning in 1914. Numbering started with "1" in each election through 1982. Since this made any historical reference to, say, "Proposition 4" ambiguous, a new system was adopted to number propositions consecutively from one election to the next so that, by June 1998, voters were casting ballots on Propositions 219 through 227. The state started over with a new Proposition 1 in November 1998, and in the future will begin a new cycle every ten years.

In 1975, the U.S. Congress amended the Voting Rights Act to protect the rights of non-English-speakers.[6] Subject to criteria spelled out in federal law and depending on the local population mix, ballots are provided in several languages in addition to English.

The closeness of the 2000 presidential election in Florida focused a great deal of attention on the mechanics of how votes are cast, especially when punch-cards are employed. In California, a variety of systems are currently in place. These include punch-cards, optical scanners, and Direct Recording Electronic (DRE) devices. Unlike some of the older punch-card systems, the one now in use employs a lever rather than a stylus and is considered less likely to produce hanging chads, and preprints candidates' names on the cards to reduce alignment errors.

Whichever method a county adopts must be certified by the secretary of state. Some counties encountered problems with DRE systems in the March 2004 primary. In April, Secretary of State Kevin Shelley ordered the decertification of one such system used in four counties. Among his objections was an absence of hard-copy verification of votes to serve as voter receipts and to allow for recounts in contested elections. He took this action despite complaints from county registrars, who defended the reliability of the systems, from disability rights groups, who argued that the new systems were more accessible by the visually impaired, and from advocates for non-English-speakers, since DRE systems can easily display ballots in various languages. Shelley did give conditional approval for other systems in place in ten other counties, while insisting that they would have to provide some form of paper trail.[7]

San Francisco has recently adopted a **ranked choice voting** system for city elections, a method also referred to as "preference voting," "single transferable voting," or the "instant runoff." Under this system, voters may rank their top three choices among the candidates for an office. If no candidate receives a majority among first-choice selections, the candidate receiving the fewest is dropped, and the votes of his or her supporters are transferred to the second choices of those voters. The process is continued (going to voters' third choices if the second choice has already been eliminated) until one candidate receives a majority. This approach is designed to ensure that all voters can vote their true preferences without throwing away their votes, and does not require a traditional runoff election.[8]

ABSENTEE VOTING

Mervin Field is one of the nation's most respected public-opinion pollsters. On election night, November 2, 1982, he demonstrated that even for the best in the business polling is at least as much an art as a science. Shortly after the polls had closed, he projected the winner in the California governor's race to be Los Angeles Mayor Tom Bradley. When final results were tallied, Bradley had finished a close second to Attorney General George Deukmejian. Field later explained that on election day itself, Bradley actually *had* received more votes than Deukmejian. The difference in the actual outcome was due to a change in the law regarding **absentee voting.** Until the late 1970s, a person could obtain an absentee ballot only for cause, usually an illness or an out-of-town trip. Under the new law, an absentee ballot could be obtained for any reason by filling out and mailing in a simple form that comes on the back of every voter's sample ballot. Although the change in the law had been supported primarily by Democrats—in part in the hope of improving traditionally lower Democratic voter turnout—it was the Republican Party that pushed absentee ballots harder in 1982. When these were counted, they put Deukmejian over the top. Since 2002, California has even allowed all voters to obtain permanent absentee voter status so that they no longer need to request an absentee ballot for each election. By March 2004, 2.2 million voters were signed up for permanent absentee status. Absentee voting now accounts for more than a quarter of all votes cast in state elections. A Field Institute study found that, compared to those who vote on election day, absentee voters are more likely to be Anglos, and tend to be older, more conservative, and more Republican. The same analysis found no relationship between absentee voting and gender, religious affiliation, or socioeconomic status.[9]

VOTING TURNOUT

Despite efforts to facilitate registration (through permanent registration, the motor-voter bill, and through later deadlines for registration) and voting (through multilingual ballots and relaxed absentee voting provisions), voting turnout in California has been in decline for some time. Figure 5.1 shows the trends in general elections from 1960 through 2002.[10] (Because turnout is significantly lower in midterm than in presidential elections, Figure 5.1 provides averages for two-election cycles in order to smooth out the curves displayed.) The percentage of the voting age population that is registered to vote has stayed about the same for decades. Actual turnout, whether measured as a percent of registered voters or as a percent of the voting age population, has declined by roughly 20 percentage points since 1960. The rapid growth in absentee voting, and the other changes we have described, seem to have had little or no impact on this trend.

California's also fares somewhat poorly in this regard compared to the nation as a whole. In 2002, California ranked forty-second among the fifty states in the percentage of eligible adults casting ballots.[11]

FIGURE 5.1
Trends in Voting Turnout

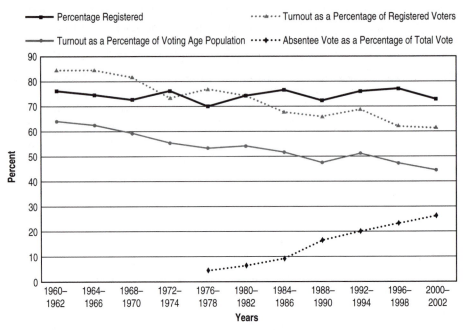

SOURCE: Derived from data in *Statement of Vote, 2002 General Election* (Sacramento: Secretary of State, 2002), vii.

ETHNICITY AND VOTING

In analyzing campaigns and elections in California, it is important to understand that, in this state, the *population* is quite different from the *electorate*. As Figure 5.2 shows, Anglos constitute about half of the total population of the state, but about seven out of every ten voters. This is because Anglos tend to be older (specifically, of voting age), are predominantly U.S. citizens, and register and vote in comparatively high proportions. The exact opposite is the case for Latinos and Asian Americans, who make up much smaller shares of the electorate than of the population. African Americans make up about the same proportion of the California population and of voters.

In recent years, the African American and Asian American percentages of voters have stayed at about the same levels while the percentage of Anglos has been declining slowly. The Latino share of the vote has been growing: from an estimated 9 percent as recently as 1994 to about 14 percent in 2000.[12] The controversy in 1994 over Proposition 187 (which, had most of its provisions not been overturned in federal court, would have restricted many governmental services for illegal immigrants) did much to mobilize Latinos politically in the years that followed. Probably more important for the long run has been the

FIGURE 5.2
Ethnicity: Population and Voting, 2000 General Election

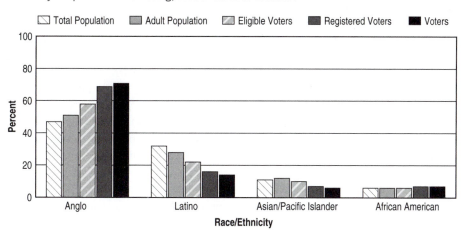

SOURCE: Based on data in "Voting in California's 2000 General Election," *California Opinion Index*, January 2002.

impact of the continuing growth in the Latino population (described in Chapter 1). The number of Latinos in the state legislature has grown rapidly. In 1998, Cruz Bustamante won the race for lieutenant governor, becoming the first Latino elected to a statewide office in California since Ramualdo Pacheco was elected to the same position in 1871.[13]

PARTIES AND ELECTIONS

Is California Becoming a One-Party State?

An essay published in 1992 by James Fay and Kay Lawson was titled, "Is California Going Republican?"[14] Though wisely cautioning that the trend might not be a lasting one, Fay and Lawson pointed to major gains by Republicans. By the mid-1980s, voters identifying themselves as Republicans had drawn even with Democratic identifiers, after having trailed badly for years.

The 1994 elections seemed to confirm Republican resurgence. For the first time in twenty-six years, Republicans won a majority of seats in the state assembly. They also gained seats in the state senate and won most of the races for statewide executive office. These gains in California mirrored national trends as Republicans won majorities in both the U.S. Senate and House of Representatives.

Since 1994, however, California and the nation have gone in sharply different directions. In the years since, Republicans and Democrats have closely contested for control of the U.S. Congress, and the popular and electoral college votes in the 2000 and 2004 presidential elections have been among the closest in decades. As noted in Chapter 1, however, Republican fortunes in California have declined dramatically, and Democrats have come to dominate recent elections at all levels.

One way to see this is by examining voting trends in state assembly races. Assembly races are chosen because they occur throughout the state every two years. They are also usually less visible than other partisan races. They are, therefore, more likely to be influenced by party affiliation rather than by the individual candidates and races, and thus more likely to reveal any partisan trends. After 1994, when they narrowly outpolled Democrats statewide in assembly races, Republicans received steadily less support through the 2000 elections, when they captured only 43.5 percent of the major party vote. Republicans did manage to improve their showing a bit (to 45 percent) in 2002.[15] Whether this, combined with Schwarzenegger's victory the following year, represents the beginning of a new trend remains to be seen. (At this writing, incomplete returns from the 2004 races indicate little change from 2002.)

In short, while California is not really a one-party state, Republicans have their work cut out for themselves if they are to again seriously challenge Democrats for supremacy.

Characteristics of Party Identifiers

Figure 5.3 shows, for each of a number of subgroups, Democratic Party strength as a percentage of those, in a survey of California adults conducted by The Field Poll in February 2003, self-identifying with one of the two major parties.[16] Democrats enjoy an edge, generally a fairly substantial one, over Republicans among all income groups except for those with household incomes over $80,000 per year. Even among members of this group, the Republican advantage is fairly modest. There are no significant differences by age, though Republicans do a little better among older respondents. As to education, Democrats do best among those with the least and with the most education, with Republicans holding a narrow edge among those with some college education.

Large differences are found when those surveyed are broken down by ethnicity. Anglos are fairly evenly divided between the two parties. Two-thirds to three-quarters of Latinos and Asian Americans identifying with one of the two major parties favor the Democrats. Identification with the Democratic Party is overwhelming among African Americans.

Little difference was found between married men and married women, or between married and unmarried men. Unmarried women, on the other hand, supported the Democratic Party by a margin of over two to one.

CAMPAIGN FINANCE

Far less money is spent on political advertising than on ads for junk food, and the money that is spent arguably serves democracy by increasing voter interest and information. On the other hand, many people, including candidates themselves, have been troubled by the need to raise large amounts of money to run for office, especially because escalating campaign costs make elected officials beholden to big campaign contributors and fund raisers.

FIGURE 5.3

Democratic Party Identification by Social Characteristics

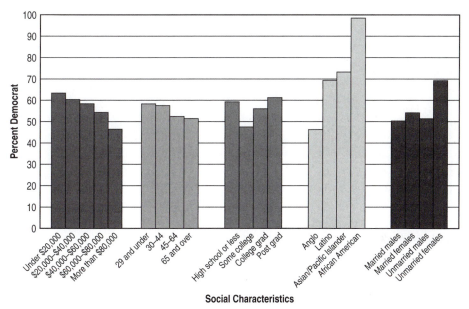

SOURCE: Analysis by author of February 2003 Field Poll.

The concern is that afterward, individuals and groups making large contributions will enjoy disproportionate access to elected officials. Some local governments in California impose stricter campaign finance limits, but for state offices there have been almost no restrictions on campaign contributions until recently, and those now in place are not very stringent.

In 1988 voters passed Proposition 73 to regulate campaign finance, but in 1990 the measure was struck down in federal district court. In 1996, Proposition 208, another campaign finance measure, was approved, but it too was declared unconstitutional in 1998. In both cases, the ruling was issued by Judge Lawrence Karlton, and in both cases he concluded that the measures had gone too far in limiting contributions and consequently violated freedom-of-expression rights guaranteed by the First Amendment of the U.S. Constitution.[17] In 2000, while Proposition 208 was still under appeal, voters approved Proposition 34, which superseded the earlier measure. Many advocates of campaign-finance reform opposed Proposition 34, hoping that 208 would ultimately be upheld and fearing that the new law was too weak. Proposition 34 does limit campaign contributions, but the limits are not as strict as those that had been imposed by Proposition 208.

The new limits certainly seem to have done little to curtail campaign spending. In 2002, contributions totaling $51.4 million were contributed to races for seats in the state legislature.[18] The following year, over $80 million was spent by various sides on the gubernatorial recall campaign.[19] As noted in Chapter 2, millions more are regularly spent supporting and opposing ballot propositions.

While this campaign slogan might seem to reflect a growing cynicism about politics, it should be noted that Senteno lost. (*John L. Korey*)

CAMPAIGN-MANAGEMENT FIRMS

Because of California's size and heavy reliance on mass media, campaigns for major office are more "air wars" than "ground wars," and depend less on personal contact and relationships and more on radio and television ads, direct mailing, and other techniques requiring the services of professional campaign managers and consultants. The traditional weakness of party organizations contributes to the need for their expertise, as does California's heavy use of ballot measures. Today, even grass roots organizations must rely on professional campaign managers in their efforts to support or oppose propositions.[20] As one writer put it, "the state has long been a consultant's paradise."[21] Over a fourth of the members of the American Association of Political Consultants are located in California, far more than in any other state.[22]

California's preeminence in the field actually predates the days of television ads, opinion surveys, computerized mailing lists, and the Internet. In the 1930s, Campaigns, Inc. was founded by husband and wife team Clem Whitaker, Sr., and Leone Baxter. The basic approach that they developed remains the model for today's campaign gurus.[23]

SURFING CALIFORNIA: INTERNET RESOURCES

The secretary of state's home page contains a wealth of information on elections, election returns, campaign finance, and more. Go to:

http://www.ss.ca.gov

For information on campaign finance, go to:

http://cal-access.ss.ca.go—scroll down to the links under "Lobbying Activity."

Not yet registered to vote? Eligible to do so? You can request that a registration form be mailed to you by going to:

http://www.ss.ca.gov/elections/votereg1.html

For links to candidates' Web sites, see:

http://politics1.com/ca.htm

A growing number of campaign-management firms and firms that include campaign management among their services have their own Web sites. Here are a couple of examples (serving Republican and Democratic candidates, respectively, in partisan races):

Allan Hoffenblum and Associates: *http://www.hoffenblum.com*

Townsend Raimundo Besler & Usher: *http://www.trbu.com*

6. The State Legislature

The only difference between a democracy and a dictatorship is a strong legislature.

—Jesse Unruh[1]

L ike the federal government, and all other states but Nebraska, California has a bicameral (two-chamber) legislature consisting of an "upper" chamber (the **senate**) and a "lower" chamber (the **assembly**). While California differs from the federal government and from many other states in having an initiative process that allows laws to be enacted without the legislature's participation, the legislature enacts the overwhelming majority of state laws.

Table 6.1 provides an overall comparison between the United States Congress and the California state legislature. While the similarities are much greater than the differences, the California legislature differs from Congress in important specifics of membership, leadership, and procedures. Moreover, the state legislature has in recent years undergone dramatic changes. Term limits have sharply increased turnover and redistributed power both within the legislature and between the legislature and other political actors and institutions.

REDISTRICTING

Every ten years, following the U.S. Census, the state legislature draws up **redistricting** plans for itself, for California's seats in the U.S. House of Representatives, and for the state Board of Equalization. These plans, which define the boundaries of each district, are enacted through the usual legislative process.

Because so much rides on the outcome, not only for the state as a whole but also for the careers of individuals voting on the plans, battles over redistricting usually have been hard fought, often bitter, and until they are resolved have consumed much of the legislature's energies and attention. As a result, there have been recurring attempts to

TABLE 6.1

Comparison of Federal and California Legislatures

	U.S. Congress		California Legislature	
	Senate	House of Representatives	Senate	Assembly
Number of voting members	100	435	40	80
Term of office (Years)	6	2	4	2
Term limit	None	None	2 terms (8 years)	3 terms (6 years)
Presiding officer	Vice president	Speaker	Lieutenant governor	Speaker

take the job away from the legislature and give it to a redistricting commission, an approach used in some other states.[2] Several attempts to create such a commission have been rejected by the voters. In 1982, Proposition 14 was defeated; two years later Proposition 39 met the same fate; and in 1990 voters turned down two redistricting initiatives, Propositions 118 and 119. All of these proposals were generally supported by Republicans and opposed by Democrats, hardly surprising given Democratic control of the legislature throughout this period. Some proposals have also been backed by nonpartisan, "good government" groups. Common Cause was a prime backer of Proposition 14, and the League of Women Voters backed Proposition 119.

After two of the past four censuses, the state supreme court has had to step in to break a deadlock over redistricting between the legislature and the governor. Following the 1970 U.S. Census, the court adopted its own plans after Republican Governor Ronald Reagan vetoed those proposed by a legislature controlled by the Democrats. In 1981, Democrats held both branches of government and were able to control redistricting. In an unusual move, Republicans put petition referendums on the ballot to overturn the Democrats' plans. Voters supported these referendums, along with one to overturn the Democrats' redistricting plan for California's congressional delegation. Ruling that there would not be enough time to draw up new plans for the next election, the California Supreme Court allowed the overturned plans to be used in 1982. For 1984, the legislature passed a new set of plans very similar to those that had been overturned by the voters. These plans, which were designed to favor the Democrats, remained in effect for the rest of the decade.

Following the 1990 U.S. Census, Republican Governor Pete Wilson and the legislature, controlled by the Democratic Party, were unable to agree on redistricting plans. As it had under similar circumstances two decades earlier, the state supreme court then imposed a plan of its own. An interesting feature of the two court-drawn plans was that assembly districts were "nested" within senate districts, that is, each senate district was divided into two assembly districts.

With the approach of the 2000 U.S. Census, both parties were keenly interested in who would control the next round of redistricting, scheduled to take place in 2001. Following Democrat Gray Davis's election as governor in 1998, Republicans qualified Proposition 26 for the March 2000 ballot. This measure would have provided for a redistricting commission and would also have resulted in a reduction of legislators' salaries. In a highly unusual move, the California Supreme Court ordered the measure removed from the ballot on the grounds that it violated the state constitution's "single subject" requirement for initiatives. With Democrats now controlling both the governorship and the state legislature, the way seemed clear for them to control the drawing of district lines that would be in effect from 2002 through 2010. Republicans feared a partisan **gerrymander,** a districting plan that would maximize the number of Democratic-leaning districts.

Instead, Democrats reached an agreement with Republicans that resulted in bipartisan plans that protected almost all incumbents from both parties. One reason for this was concern that an overly ambitious attempt to carve out more Democratic-leaning districts could backfire, since a small shift of voter sentiment favoring Republicans could result in a switch of a number of seats into the Republican column. (This is just what had happened in some states after the 1990 Census, and contributed to the Republican majority in the U.S. House of Representatives after the 1994 elections.) Democrats also sought Republican cooperation in order to head off any attempt at petition referendums. As a result of the plans that are now in place, very few districts in either the state legislature or in California's congressional delegation are considered competitive. Barring a major shift in the balance of voter support for the parties, the great majority of seats are likely to be safely in the hands of one party though 2010.

In response, gadfly Ted Costa (the same person who initiated the 2003 recall of Governor Davis) drew up yet another proposal to create a reapportionment commission, in this case consisting of three retired judges. He is attempting to garner enough signatures to qualify for the ballot in 2006. This time, however, he may get little support from either party, since both Democratic and Republican incumbents are generally quite happy with the current arrangement.[3]

Even without any gerrymandering, Democrats tend to enjoy an advantage in legislative races. In 2004, for example, they won less than 55 percent of the major party vote cast in assembly races, but 48 (60 percent) of the assembly's seats. Partly this is because, for somewhat technical reasons, a bonus of seats over votes for the majority party is typical in winner-take-all electoral systems even when no effort is made to produce this result deliberately.[4] Also benefiting Democrats is the fact that it usually takes fewer votes to win in Democratic districts. This is because such districts tend to have more residents who are minors or noncitizens, and because turnout in Democratic districts tends to be lower among those eligible to vote. Preliminary returns showed that an average of 128,000 voters participated in the 2004 assembly elections in districts won by Republicans; the comparable figure for districts in which the Democratic candidate won was only 108,000.[5] *Sacramento Bee* columnist Daniel Weintraub points out this difference in turnout to explain why Democrats have dominated the legislature, while Republicans have done much better in statewide races, where a vote is of equal importance no matter where it is cast.[6]

MEMBERSHIP

The senate has forty members elected for staggered four-year terms (that is, with half of the seats in play at each general election). The term of office for the eighty-member assembly is two years.

At one time, the California legislature was highly regarded; in 1971 it was rated the most "effective" in the nation by the Citizens Conference on State Legislatures.[7] In recent years, few observers would describe its performance in such glowing terms. One called it "nearly dysfunctional."[8] There are many reasons for this diminished image. Since the mid-1960s, California has often had divided government, with Democrats controlling the legislature and Republicans the governorship. Furthermore, the rule (discussed in Chapter 10) requiring a two-thirds vote of the membership in each chamber for passage of the state budget has frequently produced gridlock; each party has been strong enough to block the other, but neither has been strong enough to govern by itself. Although the initiative process provides a safety valve for voters frustrated with inaction, it also may contribute to the very problems it is designed to solve; successful initiatives lock in very specific policies and make it difficult for the legislature to deal with the policies' unanticipated consequences. Sharp ideological divisions between very liberal Democrats and very conservative Republicans have made cooperation across party lines difficult. Finally, runaway campaign costs continue to feed cynicism about the governing process.

Although it may not be fair to blame the legislature's shortcomings on the flaws of individuals rather than on institutional problems, legislators themselves have in fact borne the brunt of the criticism. Hoping to "throw the rascals out," voters in 1990 approved Proposition 140, imposing term limits on state legislators (as well as statewide executives). California was one of the first states, along with Colorado and Oklahoma, to adopt limits for state legislators. A total of fifteen states now have such limits.[9] Members of the assembly may now serve for a maximum of three two-year terms and senators for a maximum of two four-year terms. Proposition 140 also severely limited future legislators' retirement benefits and sharply limited the amount of money that could be spent on staff salaries and other expenses of operating the legislature. Advocates hoped that term limits would bring a return of citizen-legislators more in touch with their constituents. Opponents feared that high turnover would leave inexperienced lawmakers at the mercy of lobbyists and bureaucrats.

Do not confuse state legislative term limits with congressional term limits. Along with a number of other states, California imposed term limits on its representatives in the United States Congress when voters approved Proposition 164 in 1992. In 1995, the U.S.

Supreme Court declared such congressional term limits unconstitutional. The ruling did not apply to state legislatures, and so the state limits imposed by Proposition 140 still stand.

The impact of term limits has been dramatic. Like the U.S. Congress, but unlike the legislatures of many other states, the position of California state legislator had for a long time been a career office. In 1991, members of the assembly were, on average, in their ninth year of service while the average senator was serving his or her tenth year.[10] The fact that maximum tenure is now less than what the average was just a few years ago has had a major impact on how members think about their careers. For example, while the assembly had long been a steppingstone to the state senate, the process has been accelerated both by the push of assembly term limits and by the pull of more frequent openings created by senate limits. Although opportunities to move up to the state's congressional delegation occur fairly infrequently, state legislators are more anxious to take advantage of them when they do.[11]

The rapid rise of Hilda Solis, a Democrat from the San Gabriel Valley, illustrates these points. In 1994, she moved on to the senate after only one term in the assembly. Six years later, and two years away from being term-limited in the senate, she won election to the U.S. House of Representatives. Before winning the general election, she defeated Marty Martinez in the primary, making him one of only three incumbents nationwide to lose a primary race for the House of Representatives in 2000. Among other unusual career moves inspired by term limits was the exchange of seats in 2000 between Republicans Rico Oller and Tim Leslie. Term-limited in the Senate that year, Leslie ran for and won in Oller's assembly district (nested within Leslie's senate district) while Oller, with two years to go before he faced his own term limit in the assembly, won Leslie's senate seat.

The California legislature is a very different place now from what it was in 1990, when term limits were adopted.[12] Among its 120 members are at least five who are openly gay men or lesbians. In the 2003–2004 session of the legislature, there were thirty-six women, compared to eighteen in 1989–1990, and twenty-seven Latinos, up from seven. (By now, of course, most of these changes would have occurred even without term limits.)

The impact of political geography on representation of ethnic groups is a bit complicated because some groups are more concentrated geographically than others and because some have higher rates of voting turnout.

For a number of years, African Americans were heavily concentrated in the inner cities of the Los Angeles and Bay areas. This proved an advantage in legislative representation, since it was fairly easy to draw up districts that elected African American representatives. With the growth of the African American middle class, a decline in housing discrimination, and the influx of Latino and Asian American immigrants into the inner cities, the African American population has become significantly more dispersed in recent years. As a result, African American legislators have faced new challenges at the polls, and the number of African Americans in the state legislature declined by a third (from nine to six) since 1990. The only districts currently represented by African Americans have large concentrations of African American voters, but growing numbers of Latinos and Asian Americans. In all but one of these districts, in fact, there were more Latinos (though not necessarily Latino *voters*) than African Americans by the time of the 2000 census.[13]

Many of the rapidly growing number of Latinos in the legislature represent predominantly Latino constituencies, although some come from districts in which Latinos are a distinct minority. As we saw in Chapter 5, Latinos make up a much larger percentage of the population in general than of the number of voters. Since legislative districts are drawn up based on total population rather than voting population, it takes fewer votes to win an election in a heavily Latino district. As a result, though the percentage of legislators who are Latino is still short of the Latino percentage of the population, it actually is now higher than the percentage of voters who are Latino.

Because Asian Americans are neither as numerous as Latinos nor as heavily concentrated geographically, there are as yet no districts in which Asian American voters are a majority. When Asian Americans have been elected to the state legislature (six were serving in the assembly in 2003–2004), it has been with the support of mostly non–Asian American voters. As California's ethnic mosaic becomes increasingly complex, this may be the preferred strategy for candidates of all ethnic backgrounds. *Sacramento Bee* columnist Daniel Weintraub suggests that identity politics may give way to coalition politics, with legislators providing effective representation for constituencies that may be quite different in ethnic background from themselves.[14]

LEADERSHIP

The Assembly: Jesse, Willie, and the Strong Speaker Era

The **speaker** is the assembly's presiding officer. Although the position is still extremely important, recent events have ended the era of its peak political power in the assembly, and in state politics generally, for the foreseeable future. This peak began when Democrat Jesse Unruh became speaker in 1961 and ended when Willie Brown, also a Democrat, stepped down from the position in 1995. Their careers contain some striking parallels.

Jesse Marvin Unruh was born in 1922, one of five children in a poor Kansas family. In 1929, the family moved to Texas. An exceptionally bright child, he was ridiculed by playmates because of his large size and the fact that he spoke with a lisp. After service in the U.S. Navy during World War II, he moved to southern California. Elected to the assembly in 1954, he became speaker in 1961, winning office with significant Republican help.[15] The position had already been one with a great deal of formal authority, but under "Big Daddy" Unruh[16] it was transformed into what was "usually considered the most powerful position in the state next to the governor."[17] By the time he lost the speakership to Republican Robert Monaghan after the 1968 elections, Unruh had been speaker longer than anyone in California history.

Monaghan served as speaker for only two years. The office was held through the 1970s by two Democrats, Bob Moretti (1971–1974) and Leo McCarthy (1974–1980).[18] Though not the dominant figures Unruh had been, they maintained the position of speaker as a central figure in California's political power structure.

William Lewis Brown, Jr., was born in 1934, one of five children in a poor Texas family. An exceptionally bright child, he grew up facing the daily cruelty visited upon African Americans in the rigidly segregated old South. After graduation from high school, he moved to northern California. Elected to the assembly in 1964, he became speaker in 1980, winning office with significant Republican help.[19] He was able to make the speakership an even more important office than it had been. In the process he became arguably the most powerful state legislator in the United States.[20] By the time he stepped down in 1995, he had surpassed Unruh's record for longest tenure as speaker.

Richard Clucas argues that, in addition to the personal skills of Unruh and Brown, the era of powerful speakers was a consequence of three factors.[21] The first was the growing professionalism of the state legislature. Beginning in the 1950s and culminating with the passage of Proposition 1A in 1966, the legislature was transformed from a body of part-time, low-paid, poorly staffed members to a highly professionalized institution. The speaker's role was enhanced because the legislature as a whole was more important and prestigious than before and because the speaker controlled many of the new resources, especially the appointment of staff.

A second factor had to do with the speaker's role as leader of the majority party in the assembly. This role is not as firmly institutionalized as it is in the U.S. House of Representatives, where the speaker has for many decades been chosen almost entirely along

Assembly Speakers Willie Brown (who served from 1980 until 1995, left) and Jesse "Big Daddy" Unruh (1961–1968, right). *(© photo by Rich Pedroncelli)*

party lines. We've already noted that both Unruh and Brown came to power through bipartisan coalitions. Both went on, however, to become highly partisan leaders of the Democratic majority. California has become quite polarized along party lines in recent decades. It will be shown later in this chapter that this polarization is very much a fact of life in California's legislature. Unruh and Brown were able to use their position as leader of the majority party both to consolidate their power and to unite the majority party (and, indirectly, to unite Republicans in opposition).

The third factor that enhanced the power of the speaker was the growth in campaign costs that has occurred in recent years. Unruh himself once famously noted that "money is the mother's milk of politics."[22] Speakers were able to raise huge sums of money in campaign contributions from a variety of interests. By generously sharing this money, they placed other members, almost literally, greatly in their debt. Jesse Unruh was a skilled fund-raiser. Even before becoming speaker he had become, as one writer put it at the time, "a one-man collection agency, spreading the lobbyists' largesse among deserving Democrats for their campaign chests."[23] Most of the increase in campaign costs, however, occurred after Unruh left office. His successors in the 1970s became increasingly adept at using fund-raising to consolidate their power. It was Brown, however, who fully mastered the technique, raising far more than his predecessors had.[24]

Brown's reign was due to end in 1996 as a result of term limits. Indeed, evicting him from the speaker's chair was part of the motivation behind the term-limit movement in California. His departure was hastened, though not as quickly as his opponents hoped, by the 1994 elections. By a margin of 41 seats to 39, Republicans won a majority of assembly seats for the first time since the elections of 1968. They were poised to elect their leader, Jim Brulte, as speaker. Brown, however, was able to outmaneuver the Republicans and hold power a bit longer.[25]

First, he persuaded Republican Paul Horcher to break ranks and vote for him instead, creating a 40–40 deadlock between Brown and Brulte. Several weeks later, the assembly voted to disqualify Republican Richard Mountjoy (who had won a special election to the state senate but who had not yet resigned from the assembly). This allowed Brown to be reelected as speaker by a 40–39 margin. Republicans countered with a successful recall against Horcher. Brown and his fellow Democrats then threw their support behind Republican Doris Allen and, with their vote and hers, elected her speaker. With Allen having almost no support within her own party, Brown continued to be the real assembly leader. Several months later, Allen resigned as speaker (and was, like Horcher, soon recalled from office). Brown was then able to persuade Republican Brian Setencich to defect. Setencich, like Allen, became speaker with almost no support among his fellow Republicans.

With Brown leaving the assembly to run successfully for mayor of San Francisco, Republicans were finally able to oust Setencich in early 1996 and have a speaker of their own choosing, Curt Pringle. He would enjoy his position for less than a year. In the November 1996 elections, Democrats regained a majority in the assembly and proceeded to elect Cruz Bustamante as speaker. Both Horcher and Setencich later went to work in Brown's administration in San Francisco.

In the three years after Brown left the speakership in 1995, there were as many occupants of the position (five) as there had been during the thirty-four years of the Unruh-Brown era. The immediate cause of most of this turnover was the Republicans' razor-thin majority in 1995–1996, combined with disunity in Republican ranks and Brown's skill in exploiting this disunity. In the long run, term limits appear to guarantee that no future speaker will be able to build the kind of long-term power base enjoyed by Willie Brown during his lengthy tenure. From 1996 though 2004, a series of speakers were elected in their sophomore terms, and each retained the position for only about two years. In 2004, freshman Fabian Nuñez became speaker and can, barring the unforeseen, look forward to a somewhat longer tenure than his immediate predecessors.

The speaker still enjoys formidable powers, although for a shorter period of time. Most important of these are the right to appoint from both parties the members of all standing committees except the Rules Committee, the right to appoint five of the eight members of the Rules Committee, and the right to appoint the chairs of all standing committees, including Rules.[26] Even a specific bill in committee can be helped or hurt by the speaker, who can change committee assignments for a single day to ensure that the bill receives the desired treatment.[27] By contrast, in the U.S. House of Representatives each party is responsible for its own committee assignments; the Speaker of the House has a great deal of influence over assignment of majority party members to committees and over selection of committee chairs, but for the most part cannot make these decisions alone.[28] Once a member of the House is assigned to a committee, reassignments are seldom made except at the member's request.

In addition to vigorously exercising these formidable formal powers, recent speakers have also continued to cement the loyalties of fellow party members through aggressive fund-raising on their behalf. Although Proposition 34 limits the amount of money that one candidate can transfer to another, the speaker and other legislative leaders are still able to use their clout to encourage contributors to donate to their colleagues.[29]

The Senate

The lieutenant governor is the official president of the senate, but (much like the vice president in the U.S. Senate) has little power, votes only in the case of a tie, and usually does not even bother to show up for senate sessions. The most powerful position in the senate is that of **president pro tempore** (or "president pro tem"), that is, acting president. The significance of this position comes from the fact that the president pro tem chairs the five-member Rules Committee, which includes three members of the majority party (including the president pro tem) and two members of the minority party. The Rules Committee, among other things, appoints members from both parties to all other senate committees, and names each committee chair.[30] In recent years, rapid turnover in the speakership of the assembly has enhanced the power of the senate's president pro tem. John Burton, who served in that capacity from 1998 to 2004, came to be regarded as second in power in Sacramento only to the governor.[31] His successor, Don Perata, will be eligible to serve through 2008. His chief rival for the position was Martha Escutia, due to be term limited in 2006. Perata's longer potential tenure as pro tem was a factor in his victory.[32]

LAWMAKING

In broad outline, the process whereby a major piece of legislation goes through the California legislature (illustrated in Figure 6.1) is similar to what happens in the United States Congress. A bill can be introduced in either chamber by a member. It then is sent to one or more **standing committees** for hearings. If reported out of committee, the measure then goes to the floor for consideration. The same process is repeated in the other chamber. If the bill passes both chambers, but in different form, and if neither chamber will agree to the other's version, a **conference committee** (not shown in Figure 6.1) is appointed to try to work out a compromise. If the bill is approved by both chambers, it is then sent to the governor. A veto by the governor can be overridden by a two-thirds vote of each chamber.

FIGURE 6.1
How a Bill Becomes a Law

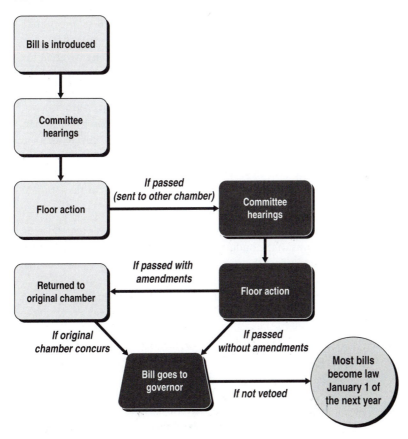

SOURCE: "How a Bill Becomes Law." Legislative Counsel, (15 June 1998) *http://www.leginfo. ca.gov/bil2lawd.html.*

There are, however, a number of important differences between the federal and state processes:

- In the California legislature, it is common for a few chairs of standing committees to be members of the minority party. In the 2003–2004 legislative session, one of twenty-nine standing committee chairs in the assembly, and three of twenty-four in the senate, were Republicans. In the U.S. Congress, committee chairs are almost always members of the majority party.

- In the California legislature, passage of a bill requires a majority of the total membership. In the U.S. Congress, a majority only of those present and voting is required.

- In California, most bills go into effect on January 1 of year following passage. In the U.S. Congress, a new law goes into effect immediately or whenever specified in the legislation. In California, for a measure to go into effect immediately, it must contain an "urgency" clause, and must pass by a two-thirds vote of the membership of each chamber.

- In the California legislature, the role of a bill's author is more central than is typically the case in Congress. Following service as a legislative staff member and subsequent interviewing of a number of members, William Muir wrote that "In no starker way did the Sacramento legislature contrast with Congress than in the critical importance of the author system."[33] By the "author system," Muir is referring to the prominent role played by the person who introduces a bill. In California, the author must negotiate the bill's passage through the entire process of committee hearings and deliberations, floor debate, consideration by the other house, conference committee, and eventual signing into law by the governor. In Congress much of this work would be handled by committee and party leaders. The California process has been criticized as inefficient and would certainly not be feasible in Congress with its 100 senators and 435 voting members of the House of Representatives.

- The governor of California possesses the item veto, that is, the power to reduce or eliminate individual line items in the budget bill or any supplemental appropriations legislation without having to reject the entire bill. At the federal level, the president did not have similar authority until a new law was passed in 1996, and the U.S. Supreme Court declared this law unconstitutional just two years later.

THE ROLE OF PARTIES

In spite of the Progressives' success in weakening California parties as organizations (discussed in Chapter 4), the state legislature has become a highly partisan institution, in which it is quite typical for votes on pending legislation to be cast largely along party lines. Figure 6.2 displays voting records of legislators in terms of "conservatism," with

FIGURE 6.2

Roll-Call Voting in the California Legislature: Conservatism Index

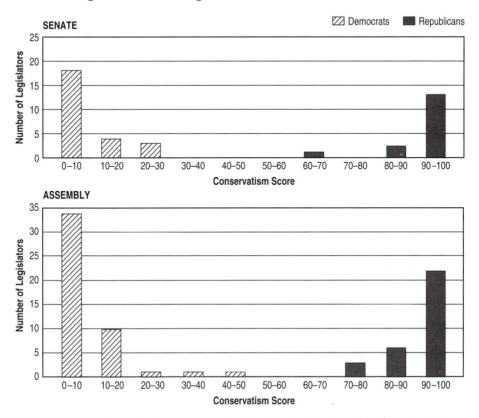

SOURCE: Composite indexes based on 2003 ratings by the California Chamber of Commerce, the California Taxpayers' Association, the California Public Interest Research Group, and the American Association of University Women–California.

the most liberal members in each chamber having scores of 0 and the most conservative having scores of 100. Scores are based on ratings for 2003 by four interest groups (two of them conservative and two liberal).[34] Not only was the Democratic Party to the "left" of the Republican Party, but there was no overlap between the two distributions.

To be sure, there are some divisions within the parties. For example, Democrats who made up the Assembly Moderate Caucus had an average conservatism score of 15, compared with an average score of about 2.5 for the liberal Democratic Study Group.[35] However, these distinctions pale by comparison with differences between the parties: the average conservatism score for all assembly Democrats was 7, compared with 92 for assembly Republicans.

Sharp ideological divisions between the parties did not always characterize California's legislature. A now classic study once labeled California the "deviant case" because of the relative absence of partisanship in its legislature as compared to other states during much of the first half of the twentieth century. By the 1950s, however, this had begun to change.[36]

Partisan voting in the state legislature is rooted in the differences between Democrats and Republicans among voters, which were described in Chapter 4, and in the rise of strong, highly partisan leaders like Unruh and Brown, discussed earlier in this chapter. Additional factors include the development in the 1950s of a genuine two-party system in the state legislature. Although the two parties had competed on fairly even terms for seats in California's congressional delegation since the New Deal, the Republican Party dominated the state legislature until the 1950s. In 1958, Democrats became a majority in the assembly and state senate for the first time in the century.

A related development was the abolition of **cross-filing,** for years one of the most effective party-weakening devices. Yet another legacy of the Progressive Era, cross-filing weakened parties by allowing a candidate to run in both the Democratic and Republican primaries (and those of minor parties as well). It was not at all uncommon for candidates, especially incumbents, to win both primaries, making a general election unnecessary. In 1952, voters approved a referendum modifying cross-filing by requiring that candidates' party affiliations be listed on primary ballots. This change, implemented in the elections of 1954, resulted in a dramatic decrease in the successful use of cross-filing,[37] and in 1959 cross-filing was eliminated completely.

Another change was the "one person, one vote" rule mandated by the U.S. Supreme Court in the early 1960s. In California, this had far and away the greatest impact in the state senate. The senate had been extremely "malapportioned," with no county allowed more than one of the body's forty seats. This meant that Los Angeles County, which at that time had about 38 percent of the state's population, possessed only 2.5 percent of the representation in the senate. The shift in representation in the senate from rural to metropolitan areas also meant a shift from areas in which the two major parties had basically similar constituent bases to areas in which Democrats represented inner cities and Republicans outlying suburbs.[38]

Yet another factor binding members of each party in the state legislature together is the fact that, along with the governor, the legislature is responsible for redistricting. Members of each party are motivated to stick together and work to put, or keep, their party in the majority.[39]

BACK TO THE FUTURE?

In many respects, the California legislature is more like Congress than it is like the legislatures of most other states. Like Congress, but in common with the legislatures of only a handful of other states, the California legislature meets on a more or less year-round basis. Members receive more and better professional staff assistance than their counterparts in other states. The pay of California legislators ($99,000 per year plus $121 for each day the legislature is in session) easily exceeds that of any other state.[40] Using a measure that combines salary, length of sessions, and staff support, Peverill Squire rates California's the most "professionalized" of all state legislatures.[41]

Recently, some have argued that California would be better off if the legislature returned to the part-time body of "citizen lawmakers" that existed prior to 1966. If this were to happen, it would, like term limits, weaken the power of the legislature to the benefit of the executive branch. Within the legislature, however, it might actually tend to concentrate power. In a number of states that currently operate with part-time legislatures, there are "executive councils" consisting of a small number of leaders who function on a more year-round basis and who tend to acquire much more knowledge and influence than their colleagues.

SURFING CALIFORNIA: INTERNET RESOURCES

There are four official sites for California's legislature:

> General: *http://www.leginfo.ca.gov* and *http://www.legislature.ca.gov*
>
> Senate: *http://www.senate.ca.gov*
>
> Assembly: *http://www.assembly.ca.gov*

The library at San Diego State University has a useful guide to tracking California legislation at:

> *http://infodome.sdsu.edu/research/guides/gov/capolicy.shtml*

Some of the information in this guide is specific to SDSU. Check with a reference librarian for the locations of materials at your campus library.

For legislative district maps, see:

> *http://www.calvoter.org/maps/index.html*

Don't know who represents you in the state legislature? For names and other information go to:

> *http://www.vote-smart.org*

7. The State's Plural Executive

[The California state bureaucracy is] a mastodon frozen in time.
—Arnold Schwarzenegger[1]

*T*his chapter will look at the elected officials who together head the state's executive. We will also examine how the executive branch of government as a whole is organized.

GOVERNOR

Thad Beyle compares the governors of the fifty states in terms of six "institutional powers": number of separately elected officials, tenure potential, appointment power, budget power, veto power, and control of the legislature by the governor's party.[2] Each of the six areas is rated on a scale of one to five, with five indicating the most power. Applying each of these categories to the governor of California provides a basis for assessing the office's strengths and limitations in comparison with those of other states.

Separately Elected Officials

Harry Truman once remarked of the presidency of the United States that "the buck stops here." This really cannot be said in the same way of the governors of the fifty states, including California, since all states to one degree or another have "plural" executives. In California there are a dozen elected executives: the **governor**, the **lieutenant governor**, the **attorney general**, the **secretary of state**, the **insurance commissioner**, the **superintendent of public instruction**, the **treasurer**, the **controller**, and the **Board of Equalization** (which includes the controller and four other members). Each is elected in nonpresidential election years to four-year terms. Each can serve in the office for a maximum of two terms. Each is answerable directly to the voters. On Beyle's five-point scale, California governors, along with those of eight other states (this and other ratings were as of 2002) received the lowest score of one.

Tenure Potential

In California and in every other state except New Hampshire and Vermont (where governors serve two-year terms), a governor is elected for a term of four years. In 1990, Proposition 140, in addition to placing term limits on state legislators, limited governors and most other elected state executives to a maximum of two terms.[3] The situation in California is fairly typical in this respect; all but fourteen states now have some form of term limit for governors.[4] On Beyle's scale, California's governor was one of thirty-eight to receive a score of four.

Some second-term governors may find it harder to build support for their programs since they will be perceived as lame ducks, soon to be gone from the scene. More likely, the practical impact of term limits will not be great. When Earl Warren was reelected governor in 1950, he became the first and last in state history to serve more than two terms. Pat Brown, the only one to try for a third term since then, lost in 1966. On balance, governors probably gain more than they lose from the new restrictions because they are now dealing with legislators who are less experienced and less well staffed.[5]

Appointment Power

As in other states, the California governor's powers of appointment and removal are limited by the **plural executive,** with several other elected state officials heading their own departments. In addition, most state employees are part of the civil service system, and the governor has no control over their appointment or removal.

The governor's powers in this area are still weighty. The governor does make a number of key nominations or appointments to top-level "political" positions in state agencies, to various boards and commissions, and to appellate courts. The governor also makes nominations to fill vacancies in other elected state executive offices and, unless otherwise specified in a county charter, fills vacancies on county boards of supervisors. Most trial court judges initially reach the bench through gubernatorial appointment. These powers are limited by the fact that many of these positions are not filled at the sole discretion of the governor but are subject to confirmation by the legislature or, in the case of appellate court justices, by a commission and eventually by the voters. The vast majority of nominations made by the governor are approved, but there have been notable exceptions. In recent years two nominees to fill vacant state executive offices have been turned down by the legislature. The governor is also limited in that many appointees, once in office, serve fixed terms and are not subject to removal by the governor. In comparing the powers of the California governor to those of governors in other states, Beyle gave the governor of California a power-to-appoint score of 3.5, about average for all governors.

Budgetary Power

The governor sets the agenda for the annual battle over the state budget. The budget is prepared under the governor's auspices and only then submitted to the legislature for its consideration. The legislature has the ability, however, to make any changes it likes to the proposed budget. These features are again typical, and so the California governor's budgetary control, and that of the governors of all but six other states, received a score of three on Beyle's scale.

In one important sense, this description exaggerates the power of both the governor *and* the legislature. As we will see in Chapter 10, because of constitutional and statutory restrictions, much of the state budget is beyond the regular control of either branch of government.

Veto Power

The governor may sign a bill, allow it to become law without a signature, or veto it.[6] If the governor vetoes a bill, it dies unless the veto is overridden by a two-thirds vote of both the senate and the assembly.

There are two features of the governor's veto that make it an especially powerful weapon. First is the requirement that vetoes be overridden by a two-thirds vote of the *total membership* of the chamber, not just by two-thirds of those present and voting. This, combined with the high levels of party unity in the legislature described in Chapter 6, makes an override extremely difficult. In fact, a quarter century has passed since the last successful attempt (during the administration of Jerry Brown).[7]

A second key advantage enjoyed by the governor is the **item veto.** This allows the governor to reduce or eliminate any item of the state budget bill or any other appropriations bill without having to veto the entire measure.[8] Combined with the difficulty of overriding a governor's veto, this usually gives the governor the final say on budget controversies. In short, while the legislature's ability to change the budget is important, it is the governor who has the upper hand, setting the agenda at the start of the process and holding the power of the item veto at the end.

The item veto is common to most states.[9] California is one of thirty-nine states for which Beyle assigned the governor's veto power a score of five. All thirty-nine provided for an item veto and an extraordinary majority for an override.

Party Control

A governor whose party does not control the legislature may be able to block the opposition party through use of the veto but will have great difficulty getting his or her own proposals enacted. Such divided government often leads to gridlock. Divided government has become the norm in California in recent years. Since 1966, the same party has controlled the governorship and both chambers of the legislature during only fifteen years: 1969–1970 (when Ronald Reagan was governor and Republicans briefly controlled the legislature), 1975–1983 (when Democrats controlled both branches during the years Jerry Brown was governor), and 1999–2003 (when Democrats were again in charge during the administration of Gray Davis).

There are a number of possible explanations for divided government:

- All else being equal, party loyalty gives an edge to Democrats because more voters identify as Democrats. The more visible the race, however, the less likely it will be that all else *will* be equal. The more information voters have about the candidates, the less they will rely on party labels to make their choice.

- The U.S. Supreme Court's "one person, one vote" rule means that legislative districts must be approximately equal in *total population*. As we saw in Chapter 6, however, actual voter turnout is generally higher in Republican districts. In other words, in legislative races a vote cast in a Republican district is not worth as much as one cast in a Democratic district. In statewide races, on the other hand, a vote is a vote wherever it is cast.

- Democrats have at times enjoyed an advantage in legislative races as a result of their control over the redistricting process. During the 1960s and 1980s, and for the current decade, district boundary lines were drawn up by the legislature, which was controlled by Democrats and which, not surprisingly, drew lines that tended to favor that party. (In the 1970s and 1990s redistricting was done through the courts, where partisan considerations did not play as great a role.)

- Divided government may also occur because people may vote for legislators and for a governor for different reasons. Individual legislators are often judged by their ability to bring programs and services to their districts. Governors are perhaps judged more by their ability to keep overall spending levels under control and taxes low. While high levels of services and low levels of taxes may not be compatible goals, voters may be attempting to "have their cake and eat it too" by voting in legislative races for Democrats (the party normally associated with higher levels of government services) and in races for governor for the candidate of the Republican Party (usually associated with lower taxes).

Because of California's divided government, partially offset by the fact that the Republican minority in the legislature is substantial (enough to sustain vetoes, for example), Beyle's index would currently assign the California governor a score of two in the area of party control over the legislature.

Summary

California governors have considerable institutional power. They can, if the voters agree, serve for eight years, long enough to achieve a substantial agenda. They have strong budgetary powers and a very strong veto. On the other hand, they must share their power with a number of other actors, especially other elected executives.

Adding all of the components of Beyle's index of institutional power, California governors received a total score of 20.5, compared to a high of 24.5 (for Illinois, New York, and Utah), a low of 16 (Alabama), and an average for all governors of 20.7. With the same party no longer controlling both the governorship and the legislature, the California governor's current score would be 18.5, placing it somewhat below the national average. As Beyle also explains, however, formal institutional power is only part of the key to a governor's impact. As chief executive of the country's largest state, the governor of California is one of the best-known figures in U.S. politics. One measure of this is the fact that most recent California governors have received at least some mention as possible presidential or vice-presidential candidates (although only Ronald Reagan has actually been elected, or even nominated). In skillful hands, this visibility becomes a powerful tool for achieving the governor's objectives. While Governor Schwarzenegger is ineligible for the presidency because the U.S. Constitution requires that a president be a "natural born" American citizen (and Schwarzenegger is a native of Austria), he has hardly lacked for national visibility.

LIEUTENANT GOVERNOR

For the most part, this office functions like that of the vice presidency of the United States. The lieutenant governor becomes chief executive should that office become vacant. The lieutenant governor also serves as president of the state senate.

Ten lieutenant governors have gone on to become governor, three through election. The other seven did so following the death or resignation of the incumbent (although three of these went on to win election as governor in their own right).[10] However, until Davis in 1999, no lieutenant governor had won the state's top office since Goodwin Knight did so in 1953. In recent decades, Glenn Anderson (lieutenant governor from 1959 through 1966) and Mervyn Dymally (1975–1979) went on to service in the U.S. House of Representatives. Retiring from Congress in 1992, Dymally won election to the state assembly in 2002, returning to a position he first held four decades earlier. Lieutenant Governor Cruz Bustamante (1999 to present) made an unsuccessful run for governor in the 2003 recall election. He has indicated that he will not seek the governorship in 2006, but will likely run for another statewide office.

The president of the senate votes only in the case of a tie, and these are rare. Under normal circumstances, the lieutenant governor does not even bother to perform the largely ceremonial job of presiding over the state senate.

There are a few differences between the roles of vice president and lieutenant governor. Aside from serving as president of the U.S. Senate and, as someone once put it, "inquiring daily into the health of the president," the vice president's duties are determined by the president. The lieutenant governor, on the other hand, does have some additional official duties. By provision of the state constitution, the lieutenant governor serves on the Board of Regents of the University of California[11] and, by statute, on various other boards and commissions.

Candidates for president and vice president of the United States are nominated at the parties' national conventions and run as a ticket. In practice, the presidential nominee handpicks the nominee for the number-two position. The lieutenant governor is nominated by voters in a primary and runs in a separate election. The lieutenant governor, therefore, not only is independent of the governor but may not even be of the same party.

Finally, the president of the United States continues to be president even when on foreign soil. The lieutenant governor of California, however, becomes acting governor "during the impeachment, *absence from the State, or other temporary disability of the Governor*" [emphasis added].[12] This language in the state constitution, a holdover from the days of more primitive systems of transportation and communication, has been interpreted literally by the courts. For the most part, lieutenant governors have avoided taking advantage of their temporary powers, even when they and the governor have been from different parties, but there have been exceptions. Mike Curb (1979–1983) did his best to discomfort Governor Jerry Brown during the latter's frequent trips out of state.

ATTORNEY GENERAL

The attorney general is the state's chief legal officer and heads the California Department of Justice. In criminal matters, the attorney general supervises the county district attorneys (who are, however, separately elected), and attorneys from the Department of Justice represent the prosecution on appeals. The department's lawyers also provide legal representation in most civil matters in which the state is involved. The office has a "quasi-judicial" role, in that state and local agencies can ask the attorney general for an "advisory opinion" in matters of legal interpretation. Such opinions carry considerable weight but can, of course, be overruled in court. The attorney general is one of three members of the Commission on Judicial Appointments, which must approve the governor's nominations to the state supreme court and district courts of appeals. Attorneys general Earl Warren (attorney general from 1939 until 1943), Pat Brown (1951–1959), and George Deukmejian (1979–1983) would go on to become governors, and Attorney General Bill Lockyer (attorney general from 1999 to the present) is considered a possible candidate in the 2006 race. Stanley Mosk (1959–1964) left to accept an appointment to the state supreme court. Dan Lungren (1991–1999) was elected to the U.S. House of Representatives in 2004, a position he had held prior to becoming attorney general.

SECRETARY OF STATE

The most important job of the secretary of state is to serve as the state's chief elections officer. Among other duties, the secretary of state oversees the voter registration programs and voting systems maintained by county registrars of voters; certifies candidates for state and federal office and signature petitions for statewide initiatives, petition referendums, and recalls; prepares a voter information guide before each statewide election; and maintains data on registration, election results, and receipts and expenditures for lobbying and campaign finance.

For much of its history, the position of secretary of state has been a career office. Frank C. Jordan served from 1911 until his death in 1940. Three years later his son, Frank M. Jordan, became secretary of state and served until he died in 1970. March Fong Eu held the office from 1975 until resigning in 1994. With the advent of term limits, their marks for longevity seem safe. Only Secretary of State Jerry Brown (1971–1975) moved on to higher office, becoming governor in 1975. In 2004, former Secretary of State Bill Jones tried unsuccessfully to challenge incumbent Barbara Boxer for her seat in the U.S. Senate.

INSURANCE COMMISSIONER

The commissioner's job is to oversee the insurance industry. For example, rate changes must be submitted to the commissioner for approval. This was an appointive office until Proposition 103 made the office elective, as part of a rewriting of the state's insurance laws that the voters approved in 1988. One of its key supporters, controversial Assemblyman Tom Hayden (later to become a state senator), promised *not* to run for the office should the proposition pass. The first elected insurance commissioner was Democrat John Garamendi. In 1994, Garamendi was defeated for reelection by Republican Chuck Quackenbush. Although reelected in 1998, Quackenbush was later forced to resign following revelations of misuse of funds from settlements with insurance companies,[13] and Garamendi won his old job back in 2002.

SUPERINTENDENT OF PUBLIC INSTRUCTION

Unlike the contests for other elected executives, the race for superintendent of public instruction is nonpartisan. In recent years, however, the general election has ended up pitting a Republican against a Democrat. Since party labels do not appear on the ballot for this office, voting tends to follow party lines somewhat less closely than in other, overtly partisan, races.[14]

Superintendents have often been very controversial. They are regularly embroiled in such hot button issues as school vouchers and bilingual education. In 1993, Bill Honig resigned after a felony conviction for conflict of interest. Governor Pete Wilson's nominee to fill the vacancy, state Senator Marian Bergeson, was rejected by the state legislature, partly on ideological grounds and partly because, even though the office is officially nonpartisan, Democrats did not want a Republican going into the 1994 elections as an incumbent.

The powers of the office are actually rather limited. The superintendent heads the Department of Education and serves as secretary and executive officer of the Board of

Education. It is, however, this board rather than the secretary that sets policy, and the board is appointed by the governor.[15] Even as a spokesperson for the state on educational matters, the superintendent must compete to some extent with the secretary of education, an appointee of the governor.

TREASURER

The late John Jacobs referred to the treasurer of California as "one of the most powerful and important offices of government finance in the nation, if not the world."[16] The treasurer is responsible for both borrowing and investing billions of dollars annually, and is also a member of the boards of the public employee pension funds, the largest such funds in the world.[17] The office's clout comes from the treasurer's influence over how state and pension fund money is directed.

Two state treasurers, Romualdo Pacheco (treasurer from 1863 until 1867) and Friend Richardson (1915–1923) would later become governor. Ivy Baker Priest (1967–1975) had previously served as U.S. treasurer in the 1950s during the Eisenhower administration. She was followed by Jesse Unruh, who had been speaker of the assembly in the 1960s and the unsuccessful Democratic candidate for governor in 1970. Just as he had earlier transformed the speaker's office, Unruh did much to make the treasurer's post the influential position it is today. Upon Unruh's death in 1987, Governor George Deukmejian appointed a member of Congress, Dan Lungren, to fill the vacancy. The legislature, however, rejected this nomination. Lungren managed to land on his feet: in 1990 he was elected state attorney general. That same year, Kathleen Brown was elected treasurer. Four years later, she would go on to become the Democratic Party's nominee for governor, but would be defeated by Pete Wilson. Her successor, Republican Matt Fong, suffered a similar fate in 1998, losing to Barbara Boxer in that year's U.S. Senate race. Treasurer Phil Angelides (1999 to the present) is considered a likely contender for the governorship in 2006.

CONTROLLER

Before the state can pay its bills, the controller must ascertain that the expenditures are proper and that there is money in the state treasury to cover the payments. In 1992, when the legislature missed by over two months the deadline for passing a budget, the state had technically run out of money. Throughout most of the summer, many state employees, vendors, and others owed money by the state were instead paid in scrip issued by Controller Gray Davis. In 2004, Controller Steve Westly threatened to withhold payment of some bills should the state not pass a budget by the end of July, but the budget was approved just before this deadline.

The controller issues regular reports on the receipts and expenditures of state and local governments, serves as chair of the Franchise Tax Board, which collects personal and corporate income taxes, and is one of five members of the Board of Equalization.

Two U.S. Senators had previously served as controllers: Thomas Kuchel (controller from 1947 through 1952) and Alan Cranston (1959–1967). Davis (1987–1995) went on to become lieutenant governor and in 1998 won election as governor.

BOARD OF EQUALIZATION

In addition to the controller, the Board of Equalization includes four other members selected from districts drawn up by the legislature after each census. The board is responsible for collecting various taxes, the most important of which is the sales tax. The board's name derives from its role in overseeing the work of county assessors to ensure that assessment practices are equal (uniform). Even though the state government receives very little of its revenue from property taxes, this is a significant responsibility because a number of federal and state programs include assessed property values in the formulas for dispersing funds to localities.

ORGANIZATION OF THE EXECUTIVE BRANCH

We call it bureaucracy, and our eyes tend to glaze over. The programs that we and our elected representatives pass into law, however, would mean nothing without the over 378,000 state employees, organized into a myriad of departments, agencies, boards, and commissions, who carry them into effect.[18]

Most government programs are housed in units that report, directly or indirectly, to the governor. Some report to other elected state executives, while still others are administered by independent boards and commissions. Figure 7.1 shows the organization of the state's executive branch, but don't be put off by the small print; it is included not in order to be studied, but rather to illustrate the complexity of the system.

The Governor's Personal Staff

The governor's personal staff is a relatively small group of people who perform critical tasks such as keeping the governor's schedule, planning the logistics of official activities, overseeing the work of the various units under the governor's control, reviewing candidates for appointed positions, providing legal advice, assisting in relations with other parts of the government and with the public, and even helping the governor with "foreign policy" (in the area of trade). Currently, the governor's personal staff consists of eighty-six authorized positions.[19]

FIGURE 7.1
California State Government Executive Branch

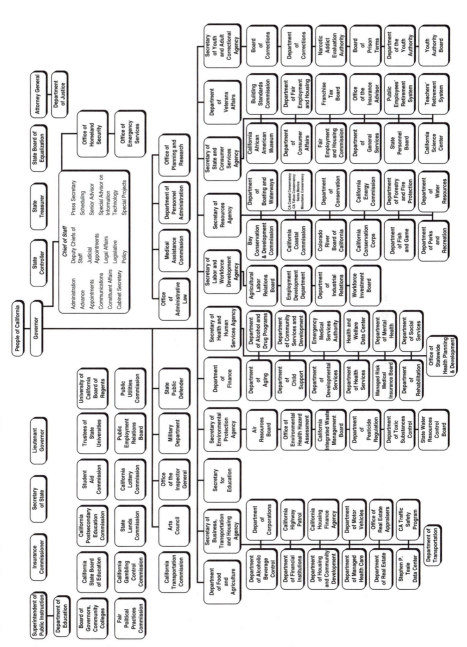

SOURCE: California Performance Review, "California State Government—Current Organizational Structure," (2004) *http://www.report.cpr.ca.gov/cprrpt/preschg/images/exhibit13.pdf* (accessed 31 October 2004). Reprinted with permission.

The "Agency Plan"

When Pat Brown became governor in 1959, he inherited an executive fragmented into twenty-one departments. To try to streamline its organization, he appointed a Commission on the Organization of State Government to study the problem. (This commission, which still exists, was also known as the "Little Hoover Commission" after similar federal commissions headed by former President Herbert Hoover.) In December 1959, the commission submitted its report calling for an "Agency Plan." Under this plan, departments were to be grouped into agencies. Each agency would be headed by a secretary. The secretaries, together with other key appointees of the governor, would form the governor's cabinet to assist the governor in coordination of programs and policies. During the course of Brown's administration, most departments were grouped under such agencies.[20]

This basic structure remains in place today. In addition to the agencies, there are several cabinet-level departments whose directors serve on the cabinet and report directly to the governor. There are other units (including the Military Department and the Office of Planning and Research) that, while not having cabinet status, for varying reasons operate outside the agency structure.

As with the president's cabinet at the federal level, there are limits on the ability of the governor's cabinet to serve as an instrument for coordination and control. Although appointed by the governor, agency secretaries and department directors are also administrators of programs. This means that, in order to function effectively, they must serve not only the interests of the governor, but also other, sometimes competing, interests as well. They administer programs authorized and funded by the state legislature and implemented by career civil servants who have their own points of view and who often serve for several administrations.

Although the overall structure of state administration has been in place for over forty years, each new governor has sought to fine tune the system. Proposition 1A, passed in 1966, increased the governor's powers of reorganization. Under legislation passed to implement these powers, reorganization plans proposed by the governor become law automatically unless either chamber of the legislature vetoes the change. On occasion, attempts by the governor to reorganize the executive have led to battles with the legislature and others. One of Governor Pete Wilson's promises during the 1990 campaign was that he would establish a California Environmental Protection Agency (Cal/EPA). Advocates of a Cal/EPA hoped that by bringing various environmental programs together under a high-level secretary, the programs could be better coordinated and more effectively carried out. Democratic Assemblyman Rusty Areias led a bipartisan coalition that sought to block the new agency. Opponents included some farm area representatives concerned that the new agency might be too restrictive in regulating toxic chemicals as well as some environmentalists concerned that the agency might not be restrictive enough. In the end, however, Areias reluctantly dropped his opposition and the governor's reorganization plan automatically went into effect.[21]

The Role of Other Elected Executives

Because the governor is only one of several elected executives in California, each member of the plural executive has separate responsibility for his or her own portion of the state bureaucracy. The Department of Justice, for example, reports to the attorney general and not, either directly or indirectly, to the governor.

Independent Boards and Commissions

In addition, some boards and commissions operate with a high degree of autonomy. In some cases (including the Board of Regents of the University of California), the powers and composition of the governing body of the board or commission are spelled out in the state constitution. Most (including the Board of Trustees of the California State University and the Board of Governors of the Community Colleges) were created by statute. The power to appoint members and the lengths of the members' terms vary from case to case.

THE STATE CIVIL SERVICE

A **civil service system** is one that awards government jobs through competition based on merit rather than through a spoils system in which politicians dispense jobs to friends and party loyalists. Civil service employees do not lose their jobs because one party has left office and another has come in. Bills to create such a system had been introduced in the state legislature as early as 1883, the same year that the Pendleton Act created the federal civil service system. In the first decade of the twentieth century, several California cities adopted their own systems, but civil service reform at the state level would have to wait until the Progressive Era. In 1913, California became the ninth state to adopt civil service.[22] Administration of the system took on its present form in 1934 and is run by the State Personnel Board. A five-member body is appointed to staggered ten-year terms by the governor with the approval of the state senate.[23] The system covers most state employees. The largest exempt categories are the employees of the University of California and the California State University, which maintain their own personnel systems.

The largest number of state employees are represented by the California State Employees Association (CSEA), which today is widely regarded as one of the most powerful interest groups in the state. The CSEA was founded in 1930 as an outgrowth of efforts by several local employee groups that had organized to push for adoption of a state retirement system.[24] In 1977, the CSEA successfully lobbied for passage of SB 839, which established collective bargaining for state workers.[25]

A small but important group of state employees who are *not* covered by civil service are political appointees. These are people in policy-making positions: the heads of agencies and departments and their top assistants. The reason for these exceptions is to enable elected officials to carry out program objectives. To do this, the people who run the programs must not be shielded from political accountability, as tenured civil servants are.

By the 1950s, there was growing sentiment in California and throughout the country that the civil service system had become inflexible. Despite the presence of political appointees, implementation of programs could not be carried out without the cooperation of key career civil servants. Since they enjoyed tenure, they could not be removed from their positions, even when they disagreed with the policy objectives of their superiors. Reformers were also anxious to develop a corps of highly talented generalists within the civil service whose careers would not become narrowly focused in a particular program specialty.[26] For these reasons, the legislature in the early 1960s passed a law creating the "Career Executive Assignment" (CEA).[27] Employees with these assignments are in a position midway between political appointees and regular civil servants. Like a political appointee, a person in a Career Executive Assignment can be removed without cause (except in cases involving discrimination based on factors such as ethnicity, gender, or party affiliation). Unlike political appointees, only those already in the civil service can apply for a CEA. Certain high-level positions are designated in the state budget for CEAs. Appointments to these positions are made from rosters of people who have qualified for such an assignment. If terminated, they have the right to return to their former classifications.

Though small in number, CEA appointees can have a significant impact. According to Nicole Woolsey Biggart, they provided a way for governors to make the **Department of Finance** "a *de facto* extension of the Office of the Governor,"[28] and thus a vital instrument for control of the budget process. The CEA concept was based on recommendations that had been made in 1955 by the federal Second Hoover Commission.[29] The federal government, however, did not itself adopt these recommendations until the late 1970s when the Senior Executive Service was created during the administration of Jimmy Carter.

STREAMLINING THE PLURAL EXECUTIVE

Many observers have concluded that the state's executive branch is needlessly complicated, diffusing responsibility and making accountability to the people more difficult. In 1996, the California Constitution Revision Commission (CCRC) recommended, among other things:

- Having the governor and lieutenant governor run as a ticket (as the president and vice president of the United States do now) and abolishing the provision making the lieutenant governor acting governor whenever the governor is out of the state;

- Making the superintendent of public instruction, treasurer, and insurance commissioner appointive rather than elective offices; and

- Combining the Board of Equalization with the Franchise Tax Board (which, among other things, collects the state income tax).[30]

The commission's recommendations, however, have been largely ignored. Another, even more ambitious attempt to reinvent state government was proposed in midsummer of 2004 by the California Performance Review, a taskforce appointed by Arnold Schwarzenegger shortly after he took office. The taskforce report included numerous recommendations, but its centerpiece called for combining or abolishing altogether over a third of the state's independent boards and commissions, and eliminating the positions of over one thousand appointees to them.[31] The report quickly came under fire from a number of sources. The legislative analyst concluded that cost savings produced by proposed reforms would fall well short of the amounts claimed by the taskforce.[32] Public employee unions objected that jobs would be privatized. Others expressed concern that elimination of many independent boards and commissions, along with consolidation of some other agencies and departments, would concentrate too much power in the hands of the governor. Still others worried that valuable programs would be gutted.[33] Whether the taskforce's proposals will have any more success than those of the CCRC remains to be seen.

SURFING CALIFORNIA: INTERNET RESOURCES

For a comprehensive index of state government agencies on the Internet, go to:

> *http://www.ca.gov*—click on "State Agency Index."

The Web sites for California's elected executives are:

> Governor: *http://www.governor.ca.gov*
>
> Lieutenant Governor: *http://www.ltg.ca.gov*
>
> Attorney General: *http://caag.state.ca.us*
>
> Secretary of State: *http://www.ss.ca.gov*
>
> Insurance Commissioner: *http://www.insurance.ca.gov*
>
> Superintendent of Public Instruction: *http://www.cde.ca.gov/eo/*
>
> Treasurer: *http://www.treasurer.ca.gov*
>
> Controller: *http://www.sco.ca.gov*
>
> Board of Equalization: *http://www.boe.ca.gov*

Interested in a career in state government? Visit Jobsmart's Web site at:

> *http://www.jobsmart.org/sacto/adjobs/govjob.htm#Calstate.*

Interested in studying public administration? The National Association of Schools of Public Affairs and Administration provides links to Web sites of undergraduate and graduate degree programs throughout the country. Go to:

> *http://www.naspaa.org.*

8. The Judicial Process

There is almost no political question in the United States that is not resolved sooner or later into a judicial question.

—ALEXIS DE TOCQUEVILLE[1]

" *I* 'll see you in court" is often far from an idle threat. More than in most societies, people in the United States are likely to turn to the courts to settle disputes. In few states in the country is this more true than in California. According to figures published by the American Bar Association and the U.S. Bureau of the Census, in 2003 there was 1 lawyer in California for every 264 people, putting California in a tie for eighth place among the fifty states in numbers of lawyers per capita.[2]

Legal disputes can be either criminal or civil. To be accused of a crime is to have allegedly committed an act that violates the public order. In a case of **criminal law,** the dispute is between the accused and the government acting on behalf of the people as a whole. This is why these cases typically have names like *"People v. Simpson."* Depending on the seriousness of the allegation, crimes are classified as felonies (punishable by death or confinement in a state prison), misdemeanors (punishable by up to a year in a local jail), and infractions (punishable only by a fine). In a suit involving **civil law,** the dispute is between two persons or sets of persons, one of whom (the plaintiff) sues the other (the defendant) claiming to have been harmed by the other's action (or failure to act) and seeking restitution. Civil cases will typically have names like *"Goldman v. Simpson,"* after the parties involved. In this context a "person" need not be a natural person but can be a business or other organization. The government itself can be a party to a civil as well as a criminal case; that is, it can sue and be sued.[3]

Figure 8.1 outlines the organization of the California judiciary. To handle both criminal and civil cases, the courts in California are organized into three levels: trial courts (called superior courts), courts of appeal, and a supreme court.

COURT STRUCTURE

Trial Courts

California's trial courts are called **superior courts.** There is one in each county. In some small counties, the superior court has only two judges, while the Los Angeles County Superior Court has 429.[4] In addition to judges, trial courts employ "subordinate judicial

FIGURE 8.1
California Court System

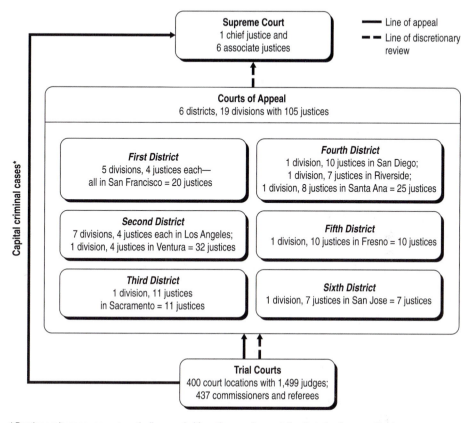

* Death penalty cases are automatically appealed from the superior court directly to the Supreme Court.

SOURCE: Reprinted with permission from Judicial Council of California, *Court Statistics Report* (San Francisco: Administrative Office of the Courts, 2000), p. xi.

officers" (such as commissioners and referees) who serve at the pleasure of the court and carry out many of the duties of judges.[5]

Until recently, there were other trial courts at a level below the superior courts. These were called municipal courts or, in rural areas, justice courts, and handled less serious cases (misdemeanors, infractions, and civil cases involving $25,000 or less). In 1994, voters approved a measure that converted justice courts to municipal courts and in 1998 agreed to another proposition allowing counties to consolidate municipal courts with the superior court. By early 2001, all counties had unified their trial courts.[6]

Because of the seriousness of felony cases, there must be an initial determination that sufficient evidence exists to warrant a trial. One way this determination can be made is through a **grand jury.**[7] There is at least one grand jury in each county. Since their principal function is to serve as a local government "watchdog," some counties have appointed a second grand jury to deal specifically with criminal cases.[8] In most counties, grand juries consist of nineteen members, though there are twenty-three in Los Angeles County, and counties with 20,000 or fewer residents may opt to have only eleven. Members are appointed to one-year terms, though a number of counties allow "rollovers" from one year to the next.[9]

Grand jury proceedings are conducted very differently from trials. The grand jury meets in closed session and hears only such evidence as the prosecuting attorney chooses to present. The defendant is not allowed to be present or to cross-examine witnesses. While this rather minimalist approach to due process may seem unfair and indeed has been criticized, the purpose of the proceedings is not to try the case, but only to decide whether a trial should be held. If the grand jury is convinced that there is sufficient evidence, it issues an **indictment,** and the defendant is bound over for trial.

Despite an increase in grand jury indictments following a 1990 change in the state constitution facilitating their use, they are employed relatively infrequently in most counties.[10] In a 2001 survey by the California Grand Jurors' Association, a number of counties reported no grand jury indictments at all over a two-year period.[11] Much more common than a grand jury proceeding is a pretrial hearing. Here, it is a judge who decides whether there is sufficient evidence to warrant a trial.

In criminal cases, "the people" are represented by the office of the county district attorney, an elected position.[12] Defendants charged with felonies or misdemeanors who cannot afford to hire a lawyer are entitled to be provided with one by the court. To meet this need, most larger counties have established public defenders offices, while most smaller counties contract with private attorneys.[13]

Except for infractions and certain types of civil proceedings, the state constitution guarantees the right to trial by jury (or **petit jury,** to distinguish it from a grand jury).[14] This right usually can be waived if both sides agree, in which event a judge decides the case. Juries consist of twelve people, although both sides can agree to a smaller number in civil or in misdemeanor cases.[15]

The jury system is based on two ideas: that the common person is as qualified as anyone else to decide questions of fact and that people who are accused of a crime or involved in a civil dispute are entitled to be judged by their "peers." The notion of a jury of one's peers (equals) dates back to the English tradition that a commoner was entitled to be judged by fellow commoners rather than by members of the nobility. In this country, it has come to mean that juries should, insofar as possible, be drawn from pools that approximate cross-sections of the public at large. Juries determine the guilt or innocence of a defendant in a criminal case. In a civil case, the jury must find for the defendant or the plaintiff. If the jury finds for the plaintiff, it must also decide how much, if anything, to award in damages. Interpretation of the law is meant to be the job of the judge, who decides on the admissibility of evidence and other procedural matters and issues instructions interpreting the law for the jury. The jury's task is to determine questions of fact based on the evidence presented.

Because the defendant is in jeopardy of loss of liberty or even life, guilt must be proven in a criminal case "beyond a reasonable doubt," and the jury's verdict must be unanimous. In a civil case, the standard of proof required of the plaintiff is lower (usually a " preponderance of evidence") and a vote of three-fourths of the jury is sufficient for a verdict.[16] In either type of case, if the jury cannot reach a verdict by the required vote, the judge will declare a mistrial. The prosecution, or the plaintiff in a civil case, must then decide whether or not to seek a new trial.

If a felony case goes to trial, the defendant's odds are not very promising. In 2002–2003, only about one in seven felony defendants won acquittal. Eighty-one percent were convicted of felonies, and another 5 percent were convicted of lesser misdemeanor offenses. Whether a judge or a jury renders a verdict makes relatively little difference.[17]

Most cases never get to trial. The great majority are disposed of before trial, usually with a guilty plea, though felony charges are sometimes reduced to misdemeanors. Civil cases, except for probate and small claims, are also normally settled "out of court."[18]

Courts of Appeal

If either side in a case believes that its rights have been violated, it may file an appeal. (An exception is that because of the "double jeopardy" clauses of the state and federal constitutions, the prosecution cannot appeal an innocent verdict in a criminal trial.[19]) Counties are grouped into six appellate district **courts of appeal,** which hear most appellate cases. In criminal cases, the Office of the State Attorney General represents the prosecution. Several nonprofit, state-funded "appellate projects" have been created to assist court-appointed lawyers representing low-income defendants in criminal cases.[20] Lawyers for each side submit written briefs (arguments), and other interested parties may submit *amicus curiae* (friend of the court) briefs with the approval of both sides or one side and the court. After briefs have been submitted, the case is assigned to a panel of three justices for a hearing.

Because it has a different purpose, a hearing before an appellate court panel is very different from a trial. The hearing is not held to settle questions of fact. There is no testimony from witnesses, and no jury is involved. Occasionally, an appellate court will rule on the question of whether a law violates either the federal or state constitution. More commonly, it will decide whether the law has been interpreted and applied correctly by the trial court and whether proper procedures have been followed.

At the hearing, the panel of justices hears oral arguments from attorneys representing both sides. After considering both written and oral arguments, the panel issues its opinion. Decision is by majority rule. A justice who is in the minority may submit a dissenting opinion. Appeals court panels usually vote to uphold the trial court.[21] Sometimes, however, the panel will reverse the trial court's decision. When it does so, it will normally send the case back to the trial court for reconsideration.[22]

The California Supreme Court

California's highest court is called the **supreme court.** The court is required to review appeals in all cases involving the death penalty. Otherwise, it generally chooses to take on only those cases that raise crucial points of law or those that have produced contradictory rulings from the different district courts of appeals. In 2002–2003, for example, the court accepted for review only 4 percent of the petitions it received.[23]

The court consists of a chief justice and six associate justices. As of this writing (November 2004), the court's membership has been unchanged since the appointment of Carlos Moreno in late 2001. Except for Moreno, the current members were nominated by Republican governors. (See Table 8.1.) Despite this, the court has not been reliably conservative in its decisions, and at least at times has been a pleasant surprise to liberals while falling short of conservatives' expectations.

Although Chief Justice Ronald George has worked hard to maintain cohesion within the court and protect its public image and its relationships with other branches of government, he has not been able to prevent sometimes sharp divisions.[24] Table 8.2 summarizes voting alignments on 83 verdicts from the time that Moreno joined the court through May 2004 in which all seven permanent members of the court participated and in which at least one justice dissented in whole or in part from the majority.[25] Figures in the righthand column indicate the percentage of times that each justice dissented. Remaining figures show the percentage of times that each pair of justices was on the same side. The table is arranged so that, insofar as possible, justices with higher agreement scores are listed closer together. This reveals at least a rough left (liberal) to right (conservative) ideological spectrum that generally coincides with commentary by court observers.[26] Joyce Kennard and Janice Brown anchor the opposite ends of the spectrum, and were the two justices most likely to be in dissent from the court majority and least likely to agree with each other. Kathryn Werdegar and Carlos Moreno tilted to the left, while Marvin Baxter and Ming Chin leaned to the conservative side. Chief Justice George was clearly the "swing" vote in the middle, least likely to be in dissent and agreeing with each of the other justices, even Kennard and Brown, on at least half of the split decisions studied.

With the possible exception of the chief justice, the member of the court who has attracted the most attention has been Janice Brown. Since joining the court in 1996, she has become known for her sharply worded dissents, sometimes to the open discomfort of George.[27] In 2003, President George W. Bush nominated Brown to a position on the Ninth Circuit (federal) Court of Appeals. Democrats, objecting to the outspoken conservatism of her opinions from the bench and in her public speeches and writings, successfully filibustered her nomination and prevented it from coming to the floor for a vote.

Disagreement within the court should not be exaggerated. Most decisions did not produce any dissents. Even when the court was divided, no justice was in dissent most of the time, and no justice was invariably either liberal or conservative. Note also that the divisions described here do not closely adhere to stereotypes about race and gender, since the court's most conservative member is an African American female.

Members of the California Supreme Court (as of November 2004). From left to right: Janice R. Brown, Joyce L. Kennard, Kathryn M. Werdegar, Ronald M. George (chief justice), Ming W. Chin, Marvin R. Baxter, Carlos R. Moreno. *(© Sirlin Photographers, Sacramento, CA)*

TABLE 8.1

The California Supreme Court

Name	Year Born	Law Degree	Year Appointed	Nominated by	Prior Judicial Experience
Janice Brown	1949	UCLA	1996	Pete Wilson	Court of Appeal, 1994–1996
Joyce Kennard	1941	USC	1989	George Deukmejian	Municipal Court, 1986–1987 Superior Court, 1987–1988 Court of Appeal, 1988–1989
Kathryn Werdegar	1936	George Washington	1994	Pete Wilson	Court of Appeal, 1991–1994
Ronald George	1940	Stanford	1991*	Pete Wilson	Municipal Court, 1972–1977 Superior Court, 1977–1987 Court of Appeal, 1987–1991
Ming Chin	1942	San Francisco	1996	Pete Wilson	Superior Court, 1988–1990 Court of Appeal, 1990–1996
Marvin Baxter	1940	Hastings	1991	George Deukmejian	Court of Appeal, 1988–1990
Carlos Moreno	1948	Stanford	2001	Gray Davis	Municipal Court, 1986–1993 Superior Court, 1993–1998 U.S. District Court, 1998–2001

*George was elevated to chief justice in 1996.

SOURCES: *Supreme Court of California,* (2004) *http://www.courtinfo.ca.gov/courts/supreme/justices.htm* (accessed 10 July 2004); A. G. Block and Claudia Buck, *California Political Almanac 1999–2000* (Sacramento: State Net, 1999), 81ff.

TABLE 8.2

| | Agreement Scores (%) | | | | | | | |
	Kennard	Werdegar	Moreno	George	Chin	Baxter	Brown	Percent Dissenting
Kennard		67	53	54	43	34	22	45
Werdegar	67		69	72	59	59	42	24
Moreno	53	69		75	57	54	40	24
George	54	72	75		75	70	51	11
Chin	43	59	57	75		83	69	19
Baxter	34	59	54	70	83		73	22
Brown	22	42	40	51	69	73		41

SOURCE: Analysis by author.

Judicial Administration

The **Judicial Council** acts as the administrative arm of California's courts. The council is headed by the chief justice of the supreme court, who also appoints an associate supreme court justice, two appellate court justices, and ten superior court judges as voting members. In addition, four voting members are appointed by the governing body of the state bar, and one each is appointed by the senate and the assembly. The council is responsible for establishing the rules governing court procedures, and makes recommendations to the governor and the legislature. In order to balance the workloads of the state's courts, the chief justice may reassign judges from one court to another. When there is a vacancy on the supreme court, or when a justice is temporarily unable for one reason or another to participate in one or more decisions, the chief justice will name appellate justices as temporary replacements.[28]

JUDICIAL SELECTION

Trial Courts

Superior court judges serve six-year terms. Elections are nonpartisan. Vacancies are filled by gubernatorial appointment, and the great majority of judges are initially appointed rather than elected. Once appointed or elected, incumbent judges enjoy high rates of success in seeking reelection. There have been notable exceptions, usually when a judge has made an unpopular decision in a widely publicized case or has been embroiled in a scandal. Overall, from 1996 through 2000, over 90 percent of superior court elections in California were uncontested.[29]

Appellate Courts

The term of office for a district court of appeals or supreme court justice is twelve years. When a vacancy occurs, the governor nominates a replacement. The nomination must be approved by the Commission on Judicial Appointments, consisting of the attorney general, the chief justice of the supreme court, and a presiding justice of a district court of appeals. Only once, in 1940, has the commission rejected a nomination.[30]

At the next gubernatorial election following an appellate justice's appointment, voters decide whether or not they wish to retain the justice for the remainder of his or her term. Similarly, at the end of a term, a justice must be approved by the voters in order to retain the office for another twelve years. In the rare event of a rejection by the voters, the position becomes vacant and the governor nominates a replacement.

Appellate justices running for reelection have almost always been successful. The only exceptions occurred in 1986, when Supreme Court Chief Justice Rose Bird and two associate supreme court justices, Joseph Grodin and Cruz Reynoso, went down to defeat. Policy differences clearly accounted for much of the criticism directly at Bird and her colleagues. The court's liberal majority had come under attack on a number of issues, notably capital punishment.

Not all of the criticism directed against the Bird court was ideological. Internal squabbles with staff and among justices damaged the court's image. One controversy involved an allegation that justices had deliberately delayed publishing, until after the election of 1978, a decision they knew would be unpopular. A subsequent investigation embarrassed the court by publicly exposing much of the often petty bickering that had been going on.[31]

REMOVAL OF JUDGES

In addition to defeat for reelection, judges at any level may be impeached and removed by the legislature or recalled by the voters. They may also be removed for misconduct by the Commission on Judicial Performance. Removal from office is mandatory for a judge convicted of a felony. Other forms of misconduct can result in removal from office or lesser penalties imposed by the commission, which can also forcibly retire a judge no longer able to perform the duties of office. The commission consists of eleven members, three appointed by the supreme court, two appointed by the State Bar Board of Governors, and six "public" (that is, nonlawyer) members appointed by the governor with the approval of the state senate.[32]

Until 1994, the commission could only recommend disciplinary action against judges to the supreme court, and had come under criticism on the grounds that it rarely did so. In response, voters in November 1994 approved Proposition 190. This measure amended the state constitution to increase the size of the commission to its present eleven members and provide for a majority of public members, to require that disciplinary hearings be public, and to empower the commission to take action itself, rather than merely make recommendations. Such actions are, however, still subject to supreme court review.[33]

Ever since the commission received the power to remove judges, it has done so on only four occasions, a rate not very different from what had existed before the proposition was approved. A number of judges, however, have received lesser forms of discipline.[34]

ACCOUNTABILITY VERSUS INDEPENDENCE

In a democracy, how responsive *should* judges be to public opinion? There are two important but conflicting principles at work in attempts to answer this question: *independence* and *accountability.*

Independence is crucial to a commitment to the rule of law in at least two ways. The first is to ensure that judges will treat each side, in either a civil or criminal proceeding, in a way that is fair and impartial. Especially in emotional and highly publicized cases, such as those that have involved child molestation, domestic violence, or racial conflict, it is important to avoid either the appearance or the reality that a judge's actions can be swayed by an inflamed public or sensationalistic media.

A second reason for judicial independence has to do with checks and balances and the courts' role in the policy-making process. In *Federalist Paper* No. 10, James Madison argued that the great test by which the success of the U.S. Constitution would be judged would be whether it could provide a system of both majority rule and protection against majority tyranny. In *Federalist Paper* No. 78, Alexander Hamilton argued that, being more protected from political pressures, courts could play a key role in checking and balancing the popularly elected branches of government. Without judicial independence, Hamilton argued, constitutional limitations on the power of elected officials "would amount to nothing."

The need for accountability can be stated simply. Courts, in interpreting statutes and constitutions, are not carrying out a merely technical task but are, of necessity, involved in deciding what constitutions and statutes actually mean in practice. In other words, they are inevitably a part of the policy-making process. In a democracy, the process of making public policy must be one that is answerable to the people.

Although it might be conceded that both judicial independence and accountability are important, the balance between the two has been resolved somewhat differently in the U.S. and the California constitutions. The framers of the U.S. Constitution, concerned about the dangers of abuse of power by the majority and their elected representatives, placed a great emphasis on judicial independence. Federal judges are appointed rather than elected and they serve until death or retirement, except in rare cases of impeachment. In California, the state constitution, while still attempting to protect judicial independence, has placed somewhat more stress than the federal Constitution has on majority rule and hence on accountability. Judges are selected through a process that involves the voters (especially at the trial court level), serve six-year (for trial court judges) or twelve-year (for appellate court justices) terms of office, and may be removed by the voters as well as by the state legislature or the Commission on Judicial Performance.

COURTS, CONSTITUTIONS, AND FEDERALISM[35]

The extent of, and limitations on, civil rights and liberties in California generally do not differ radically from what they are in all other states. This is hardly surprising since, according to the supremacy clause in Article 6 of the U.S. Constitution:

> This Constitution, and the Laws of the United States which shall be made in Pursuance thereof; and all Treaties made, or which shall be made, under the authority of the United States, shall be the Supreme Law of the Land; and the Judges in every State shall be bound thereby, any Thing in the Constitution or Laws of any State to the Contrary notwithstanding.

Thus, if a state law or a state constitution violates federal law, it will be invalidated. For example, in 2004 a California law allowing patients to sue health maintenance organizations was overturned by the U.S. Supreme Court because the Court held that this area was a matter "preempted" by federal law.

The *due process* and *equal protection* clauses of the Fourteenth Amendment of the U.S. Constitution are especially important. The U.S. Supreme Court has used them to apply to the states almost all of the restrictions that the Bill of Rights places on the power of the federal government.

There is nothing, however, that prevents a state, either in its constitution or through ordinary statutes, from providing its people with *additional* legal rights and liberties over and above those guaranteed throughout the country. The federal Family and Medical Leave Act, for examples, guarantees workers only *unpaid* leave to care for a newborn child or sick family members. California law, on the other hand, provides workers with partially paid leaves through the workers' compensation program. Many employers dislike this program, fearing its potential costs, but they can do little about it since there is no federal law to prevent the practice.

Somewhat more controversially, state courts will sometimes interpret the state constitution differently than federal courts have interpreted the U.S. Constitution even when the wording of the two documents is identical. At first glance, this might seem to contradict Article 6. At the very least, since state courts are bound by U.S. Supreme Court interpretations of the working of the federal Constitution, such courts put themselves in an awkward position when they give different meaning to the same words in the state constitution.[36]

The California Supreme Court has, on a number of occasions, asserted "independent state grounds" to interpret a number of provisions of the California Constitution more broadly than similar or identical clauses of the U.S. Constitution had been interpreted. As the court wrote in 1975:

> The California Constitution is, and always has been, a document of independent force. Any other result would contradict not only the most fundamental principles of federalism but also the historic basis of state charters. It is a fiction too long accepted that provisions in state constitutions textually identical to the Bill of Rights were intended to mirror their federal counterparts.[37]

The people of California had made this explicit the previous year when they approved a constitutional amendment that read in part: "Rights guaranteed by this Constitution are not dependent on those guaranteed by the United States Constitution."[38] Addition of this language was not seen as breaking new ground, but was part of a largely technical revision.

The U.S. Supreme Court also has recognized the "independent grounds" doctrine. Writing in 1965, the Court said that "even though a state court's opinion relies on similar provisions in both State and Federal Constitution, the state constitutional provision has been held to provide an independent and adequate ground of decision. . . ."[39]

Federal courts will accept an appeal from a state court decision only if there is a "case and controversy" over a "federal question." In other words, the person making the appeal must show that he or she has been denied something that federal law or the U.S. Constitution guarantees.

An example of the independence grounds doctrine at work is illustrated by the case of *Pruneyard Shopping Center v. Robins.*[40] A group of students had gone to a privately owned shopping center to gather petitions to be sent to the White House opposing a pending United Nations resolution condemning Zionism. They were ordered to leave by security guards and later filed suit alleging violation of their freedom of expression. Under the U.S. Constitution, they would have had no recourse. In an earlier case, the U.S. Supreme Court had ruled that "The First and Fourteenth Amendments safeguard the rights of free speech and assembly by limitations of *state* action, not on action by the owner of private property used nondiscriminatorily for private purposes only."[41]

The California Supreme Court took a very different view, holding that freedom of speech and of petition are constitutionally protected against infringement by owners of private property as well as by the government.[42] The court based its decision only in part on the fact that the language of the state constitution is more sweeping than that of the federal Constitution.[43]

The owners of the shopping center appealed to the U.S. Supreme Court on the grounds that the decision of the state court had violated *their* rights under the U.S. Constitution. They argued first that the court (an agency of the state government) had violated their right to freedom of expression by forcing them to allow the petitioners to use their property. They contended further that doing so involved a "taking" of their property in violation of the Fifth Amendment, which holds that private property may not "be taken for public use without just compensation." The U.S. Supreme Court rejected both of these arguments, allowing the California Supreme Court's decision to stand.

THE CRIMINAL JUSTICE SYSTEM

The State of California currently incarcerates about 163,500 adults in state prisons and other facilities run by the Department of Corrections. Table 8.3 describes the inmate population. The rate of incarceration is somewhat higher than the national average.[44] The California Youth Authority detains about 4,300 juvenile offenders.[45] Local jails house around 75,000 adult inmates, over 60 percent of whom are awaiting trial or sentencing.[46]

Although it has stabilized in the last few years, the state's adult prison population has grown sevenfold over the past quarter century. This has been the result of several factors, including stiffer sentences and less emphasis on rehabilitation of criminals. It has also been attributed to the state's "determinate sentencing" law, adopted in the late 1970s. Under the indeterminate sentencing rules that the new system replaced, a convict might be sentenced to a term of ten to twenty-five years, giving great leeway to corrections officials and the judiciary. The new fixed-term sentences were intended to prevent discrimination, but they also had the effect of lengthening prison stays overall.[47]

The California Correctional Peace Officers Association (CCPOA), which represents state prison guards, has become a major player in state politics, actively endorsing and supporting candidates for office in state government. The CCPOA enjoyed an especially close relationship with Governor Gray Davis, and was able to win major victories in salaries and benefits.

Recently, this success has produced a backlash. In addition to concerns about the budgetary impact of correctional officers' contracts, the entire state corrections system has been put on the defensive by a variety of developments, including:

- scandals involving abuse of prisoners by guards and fellow inmates,

- overcrowding (with state prisons housing twice as many inmates as they were designed to accommodate),[48] and

- racial conflict among inmates.

TABLE 8.3
Characteristics of Adult Inmate Population in State Correctional Facilities

Gender		Race/Ethnicity		Type of Offense	
Male	93%	Anglo	29%	Against Persons	50%
Female	7	African American	29	Against Property	21
		Latino	36	Drugs	21
		Other	6	Other	7
	100%		100%		100%

SOURCE: California Department of Corrections, "Facts and Figures," (12 August 2004) *http://www.corr.ca.gov/CommunicationsOffice/facts_figures.asp* (accessed 31 October 2004).

In July 2004, Federal District Judge Thelton Henderson warned that he might order a takeover of the system under his supervision unless it did more to address its "systemic problems."[49]

Another controversy directly affecting the state's prison system is California's "three strikes" law. In November of 1994, voters approved an initiative reaffirming a law passed earlier in the year by the legislature. This measure provided that a person with two prior convictions for "serious or violent" felonies who was then convicted for any third felony would receive a sentence of twenty-five years to life.[50] Many people came to feel that this measure was unduly harsh, since it resulted in some people receiving lengthy sentences for relatively minor offenses. In November 2004, Proposition 66, which would have modified the law to provide for a twenty-five-year to life sentence only when the third offense involved specific serious or violent crimes, and reduced the number of crimes considered serious or violent, was defeated.

SURFING CALIFORNIA: INTERNET RESOURCES

The official Web site for the California court system is:

http://www.courtinfo.ca.gov

Among other things, you can find the texts of recent decisions by the Supreme Court and the courts of appeal. You should also take a look at:

http://california.findlaw.com (free registration required)

Included at this site are decisions of the Supreme Court, including a number of less recent opinions, and links to the Web sites of California law schools and law firms.

If you're thinking about a legal career, visit the Law School Admissions Council site at:

http://www.lsac.org/

and the Hieros Gamos site at:

http://hg.org

9. Local Governments and Tribal Governments

Think globally but act locally.

—RENÉ DuBos[1]

All politics is local.

—TIP O'NEILL[2]

*P*ick up this morning's paper. Very likely there are a few stories having to do with war and terrorism, meetings of diplomats, and trade deficits. A little closer to home will be accounts of a standoff between the president and Congress, the latest Supreme Court decision, or who is ahead in the polls as we get closer to the next election. There may be an article or two about what the governor and state legislature are doing in Sacramento. What all of these stories have in common is that there is probably not a great deal that an average individual can do to influence any of these events.

Of course you can and should do *something*. You can certainly try to be an informed and conscientious voter in national and state elections. You can contribute time, money, or both to campaigns and organizations that share your goals and values and that are working to solve world and national problems. You can even pursue a career that will enable you to be politically involved directly at the state, national, or international level. The collective impact of such efforts may be enormous. Nevertheless, because the problems are so large, and the number of actors involved in them are so many, it will be hard to measure the impact of your own actions and difficult to see that you are making a difference.

At the local level, there is a contrasting difficulty: often, very few are involved. In some cases, important issues are ignored by all but a small number of people. Those who are active sometimes form small networks virtually invisible to the general public. Problems at the local level, though often defying easy solution, are of a more human scale. Great opportunities exist for those who want to make a tangible difference.

This assumes, of course, that you know something about the structure and operation of local government. This is not always easy. Although not as far away, local politics can be just as hard to see clearly as politics at the state, national, and international levels. Partly, this is because, as we noted in Chapter 3, local government is generally very poorly covered by the media. It is also very complex. D. J. Waldie, the City of Lakewood's public information officer, describes the state's local governments as "a jigsaw puzzle with more than five thousand pieces"[3] that often overlap.

LOCAL GOVERNMENTS AND THE STATE

The U.S. Constitution established a **federal** system of government: one in which sovereignty is divided between a central government and the various states, each having powers that the other cannot take away. Internally, however, California and the other states have a **unitary** form of government. All local governments are creatures of the state of California and have no authority beyond the constitution and laws of the state. In practice, however, California's many local governments operate with a considerable degree of autonomy and carry out programs and policies that have a great impact on the lives of Californians. Local governments include general-purpose governments (cities and counties) and special-purpose governments (special districts and school districts).

GENERAL-PURPOSE GOVERNMENTS

Cities

There are 476 incorporated cities in California. Over four out of every five Californians live within their boundaries. They range in population from Vernon (a busy industrial city during the day, but with a residential population of only 95) to Los Angeles, which is the nation's second largest city (behind New York) with a population of 3.9 million. The second largest city in California, and the seventh largest in the country, is San Diego, with a population of 1.3 million.[4] Eleven other cities in California (in order of size: San Jose, San Francisco, Long Beach, Fresno, Sacramento, Oakland, Santa Ana, Anaheim, Riverside, Bakersfield, and Stockton) have between a quarter of a million and a million inhabitants. Over a fourth of all Californians live in one of these dozen cities.[5]

Those living in unincorporated areas who wish to form a city must first obtain approval from the county's **Local Agency Formation Commission** (LAFCO, which in most cases is made up of representatives of the county, cities, special districts, and the general public) and by the County Board of Supervisors. If these approvals are obtained, the question of cityhood is then decided by voters living within the proposed city's boundaries. A simple majority is required for passage.[6]

The primary responsibilities of city governments can be seen from a list of city expenditures: public safety (primarily police and fire protection), public utilities (mostly water and electric), transportation (especially streets and highways), health (mostly waste management), community development (including planning and regulation enforcement), and culture and leisure (primarily parks and recreation).[7]

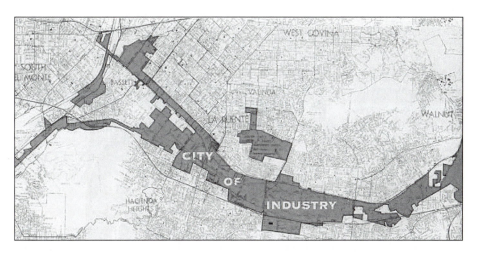

Local Agency Formation Commissions (LAFCOs) were established at least in part to prevent the creation of cities like Industry, whose odd boundaries were designed to maximize tax revenue and minimize the residential population. *(Reprinted with permission.)*

Most cities are governed by the "general law" of the state, that is, rules spelled out in the state's government code. Those desiring a bit more autonomy can, by popular vote, draw up their own charters. There are at present 88 **charter** cities.[8] Although some of these are very small, it generally follows that the larger the city, the more likely it is to have a charter. The largest **general law** city in the state is Fremont, with a population of 209,000. Charters may be amended either by initiative or by referendum.[9]

The governing bodies of cities are called city councils, most of which have five members. Most councils are elected **at large** (citywide).[10] Some use **single-member districts** with one council member elected in each.

The Progressives, who thought that council members should represent the common good of the city as a whole and not just the local interests of their part of town, favored at-large elections. More recently, at-large districting has come under attack from ethnic minorities since, if voters cast their ballots along ethnic lines, it may be impossible for minority candidates to win in citywide contests. In some cities, of course, ethnic "minorities" have become a voting majority.

The mayor of a city is usually a member of the city council. In some cities, the mayor is elected directly, while in others he or she is chosen from among council members. A few cities, including Los Angeles, San Francisco, and (as a result of a November 2004 charter amendment) San Diego, employ a "strong mayor" system in which the mayor is not a member of the council but has veto power over its decisions.[11]

Except in the largest cities, service on a city council is not a full-time job. In general law cities, maximum salaries for city council members vary by city size, starting at up to $300 per month for cities with populations of 35,000 or less, and topping out at no more than $1,000 a month for cities with over 250,000 residents.[12] All but a few cities therefore hire professional city managers to administer city staff and services.[13] Most of the exceptions are either quite large (such as Los Angeles and San Francisco) and have full-time mayors, or are quite small and have neither the need nor the resources sufficient for a city manager form of government.

City managers are typically well educated and experienced in public administration, and are paid accordingly. International City/County Management Association (ICMA) data show that, for 218 municipalities for which figures were available, the median salary of city managers in 2003 was $137 thousand.[14] Generally, though not invariably, the larger the city (and, presumably, the more complicated its administration) the higher the manager's salary.[15]

Counties

When California became a state in 1850, it was divided into twenty-seven counties. By 1907, when Imperial County was formed from the eastern portion of San Diego County, the number had increased to fifty-eight, where it has remained ever since.[16] Twenty-eight percent of all Californians live in Los Angeles County, which has a population of almost ten million. This population is more than that of any other county in the nation, and more than that of forty-two of the fifty states.[17] Another seven counties (in order of size: Orange, San Diego, San Bernardino, Santa Clara, Riverside, Alameda, and Sacramento) have populations between one and three million. Alpine, with about 1,200 residents, is the state's smallest county.

For the 18 percent of Californians living in unincorporated areas, the county is the only general-purpose local government. In three counties, Alpine, Mariposa, and Trinity, there are no incorporated cities at all. All counties contain at least some unincorporated areas except for San Francisco, where the city *is* the county.

The largest portions of county expenditures are for public assistance to needy families and individuals, for health and hospitals, and for public safety (including courts, sheriffs' and fire departments, and detention and correctional institutions).[18] Much of what county government does is to act on behalf of other units of government. Counties provide social services mandated and often paid for by the state and federal government.

As with cities, counties may choose to operate under the state's general law for counties, or they may adopt their own charters. Twelve counties, most but not all in large metropolitan areas, have chosen to do the latter.[19]

County governing bodies, called boards of supervisors, are elected in single-member districts. All boards except San Francisco's have five members, although there have been proposals to expand the board in Los Angeles County, where each member currently represents about two million people. Base salary in 2001 for members of county boards ranged from a low of less than $12,000 (Modoc) to a high of $133,000 (Los Angeles), with a median of $43,000.[20]

In addition to the board of supervisors, voters in each county elect the sheriff, the district attorney, and the assessor. Some counties provide for additional elected positions.[21]

Most counties employ a county administrator,[22] whose job and pay are similar to that of a city manager.[23]

The Special Case of San Francisco

Unique in California, although found in some other parts of the country, San Francisco has a consolidated city/county government. The City and County of San Francisco has an eleven-member board of supervisors, chosen from single-member districts, and a separately elected mayor.

SPECIAL-PURPOSE GOVERNMENTS

School Districts

In addition to an office of education in each county, California has about a thousand school districts, including elementary, high school, and unified (elementary and high school) districts, that together enroll over six million students from kindergarten through grade 12. Far and away the largest of these is the Los Angeles Unified School District, which alone has close to 750,000 students.[24] In addition, 110 community colleges in 72 community college districts enroll about 1.6 million students.[25] An elected board of education (or board of trustees), usually having five members, serves as a district's governing body.

School districts often constitute exceptions to the general rule about the low public visibility of local government. In recent years, schools have become battlegrounds between social liberals and social conservatives over a wide range of often highly emotional issues, including bilingual education, evolution, phonics, school prayer, and textbook selection. As a result, school board elections are often hotly and bitterly contested. Some issues involving the schools have moved from the local to the statewide arena through the initiative process. In Chapter 10, we will examine ballot measures that have radically altered the way in which public schools are funded. Other propositions involving educational initiatives have included unsuccessful measures in 1993 and 2000 that would have provided tuition vouchers for students at nonpublic schools.

In June 1998, voters approved Proposition 227, the "English Language in Public Schools" statute initiative. As a result of growing levels of immigration, about 25 percent of California's public school children were classified as "limited English proficient" (LEP) by the 1996–1997 school year.[26] Controversy had long been growing over whether the better way to meet the educational needs of such children was through "bilingual" education or English "immersion." Proposition 227 came down on the side of the latter, greatly limiting bilingual education and transitioning LEP students into regular classes after a year of "sheltered English immersion."

Special Districts[27]

The Turlock Irrigation District was established in 1887, becoming California's first special district. Currently, the state has close to five thousand other units of government called **special districts.** They may have been created to provide a service for a small area within a city or county, or they may cover an entire region. They may perform just one function or several. Almost seven hundred are "joint exercise of powers" districts set up by two or more general-purpose governments to deal with problems, such as public transportation or air pollution, that transcend jurisdictional boundaries.

Over 60 percent of special districts are "independent" districts. Such districts have separate governing bodies, usually elected but in some cases appointed for fixed terms by county boards of supervisors or city councils, or both. The rest are "dependent" districts in which the governing board is simply the county board of supervisors (or, much less commonly, the city council) technically acting in a different capacity, or where some members are appointed without fixed terms.

The governing bodies of some independent districts, such as special tax assessment districts, are elected by landowners, rather than by all registered voters. Although this might seem to be in clear violation of the "one person, one vote" standard governing legislative bodies in the United States, the U.S. Supreme Court has ruled that, because of its "special limited purpose and of the disproportionate effect of its activities on landowners," such an arrangement is constitutional. The court also held that, even among landowners, voting could be weighted by the assessed value of land owned.[28]

The large number and varying structures and functions of special districts result in a bewildering maze of jurisdictions. A report by the Little Hoover Commission (a government watchdog agency appointed by the governor and the state legislature) found that "special districts often operate in relative obscurity, hidden from the scrutiny of the public they were created to serve" and that "much of the public may not even realize that they are indeed governments."[29] A study by the commission of special districts in Sacramento and Contra Costa counties found that special district elections are often uncontested and that, when they are, voter participation is generally lower than in city council elections.[30] In recent years, the number of special districts has declined modestly as a result of consolidation or dissolution. In the fourteen-year period ending in 2002, the total decreased by 7 percent (from 5,108 to 4,754).

DIRECT DEMOCRACY IN LOCAL GOVERNMENT

The referendum, initiative, and recall, described at the state level in Chapter 2, also play an important role in local government. A number of key decisions by local government must be referred to voters for their approval. Matters subject to the referendum include tax increases, most bonds, and the adoption and amendment of charters.

Local initiative measures are also important. From 1999 through 2002, voters approved 23 of 36 county initiatives (64 percent). In cities during that same period, of 216 measures placed on the ballot by initiative, 105 (49 percent) passed. Another 11 measures qualified for the ballot did not go to the voters because they were first adopted by the city council.[31] (As noted in Chapter 2, this process, the "indirect initiative," no longer exists at the state level.[32])

In 1903, seven years before it was approved for state offices in California, the City of Los Angeles became the first government in the nation to adopt the recall. Despite the worldwide attention generated by the recall of Governor Davis and his replacement by Arnold Schwarzenegger in 2003, recalls are in fact far more common at the local level. Surveys of county, city, and school district elections in California from 1995 through 2002 list a total of 142 recall contests. This is one situation in which the usual incumbency advantage does not hold—two-thirds of attempted recalls were successful.[33]

CONTRACTING

Instead of providing its residents with a particular service (such as police, fire protection, or libraries) itself, a local government may contract with a private enterprise or with another unit of government for that service. Some small or medium-size cities contract with the county for a broad range of functions. This approach is called the "Lakewood Plan" after the city that pioneered the practice in 1954.[34]

There is no hard-and-fast rule as to what defines a **contract city**. The California Contract Cities Association numbers 72 members, but the Association has estimated at 115 the total number of cities that contract for major services such as police and fire protection. Contract cities are found throughout the state, but are most common in Los Angeles County, where about three-quarters of the Association's member cities are located.[35]

COUNCILS OF GOVERNMENTS

Councils of governments (COGs) were established in regions throughout the state as the result of enabling legislation passed in 1960. The oldest COG is the Association of Bay Area Governments (ABAG),[36] and the largest is the Southern California Association of Governments (SCAG), which encompasses all of southern California except San Diego County. In all, there are twenty-five COGs in California, covering (except for a few rural counties) almost the entire state. This includes one interstate organization, the Tahoe Regional Planning Agency.[37]

COGs were originally established to coordinate land-use planning and later took on other regional planning functions as well. They also coordinate federal grant applications from local governments. Since they are not governments, and lack the independent authority that regional governments would have, their principal role is to provide information and other services to their members.[38]

REORGANIZING LOCAL GOVERNMENT

Some local governments, notably in the Los Angeles area, have jurisdiction over populations larger than those of many independent countries. Many people have concluded that these entities have become remote and unresponsive and have launched unsuccessful movements to break up the City of Los Angeles and the Los Angeles Unified School District. At the same time, there are hundreds of local governments so small and obscure that many of their own residents are unaware of their existence. The California Constitution Revision Commission described local government in the state as "a confusing array of governmental entities, a number of which have overlapping, if not conflicting, duties and responsibilities."[39] This very complexity, however, makes the task of reorganizing local government to make it more efficient and accountable a daunting one.

TRIBAL GOVERNMENTS AND CALIFORNIA POLITICS

Although councils of government are not themselves governments, but are part of the state political system, something like the opposite is true of Native American tribal governments in California. *Legally*, they are not creatures of the state, but possess their own sovereignty. *Geographically*, they are located in the state, and so their members are U.S. citizens and California residents. *Politically*, they have in recent years become major players in state politics, principally as a result of tribally run gambling (or gaming) casinos. For this reason, no analysis of California politics would be complete without a discussion of their role.

Tribal governments enjoy a sovereign status somewhat akin to that of the "sovereign states." They are like states in that they have certain powers that even the federal government cannot take away, but they are also like states in that they are subject to valid federal law. (Ultimately, federal courts decide what laws are valid under the U.S. Constitution and under treaties between tribes and the United States.) In general, tribes are subject to state jurisdiction only to the extent specifically authorized in federal law.[40]

There are over 100 federally recognized tribes in California, with another 50 or so seeking recognition.[41] Typically, tribes are governed by an elected council that functions somewhat like a city council or county board of supervisors.[42]

The key political role that some tribes have come to play in recent years dates from a federal law passed by Congress in 1988. This law, the Indian Gaming Regulatory Act, authorized compacts between tribes and state governments allowing tribes to provide Class III (or "casino-style") gambling (that is, gambling involving the use of slot machines, and games such as craps and twenty-one) on tribally controlled land. In 1998, voters approved Proposition 5, a statute initiative allowing such compacts in California. When the state supreme court ruled Proposition 5 to be in violation of the state constitution (which outlawed gambling casinos in California), voters approved another measure in 2000, Proposition 1A, which amended the constitution and permitted the compacts to proceed.[43]

In recognition of the financial stakes involved, tribes spent heavily on successful campaigns to pass propositions 5 and 1A, and also became major contributors for and against candidates for office. In 2001, they helped defeat former Assembly Speaker Antonio Villaraigosa in his bid to become mayor of Los Angeles. They have also suffered some defeats along the way. In the 2003 gubernatorial recall election, they supported retention of Governor Gray Davis. On the replacement portion of the ballot, they favored Cruz Bustamante.

A large percentage of Native Americans in California and elsewhere have long suffered widespread and chronic poverty and unemployment. For a few, tribal gaming has produced enormous benefits. When a small tribe operates a successful casino readily accessible to large populations of visitors, the results can be startling. Each member of the Pechanga Band of Luiseño Mission Indians in Riverside County (within a relatively short drive from the Los Angeles, Orange County, and San Diego areas) receives approximately $10,000 a month in casino profits.[44] This is, however, far from typical. The majority of California's Native Americans have received nothing as a consequence of tribal gaming. Most are not members of federally recognized tribes, and many tribes are in locations not favorable to the operation of casinos.[45] (Tribes with gaming compacts do, however, share some of their revenues with nongaming tribes.)

The large amounts of money at stake (with total revenues estimated at $5 to $8 billion annually)[46] have provoked bitter disputes over questions of tribal membership. Some tribes have expelled families that had been considered members for many years.[47]

In November 2004, voters faced two ballot measures crucial to the future of casino-style gambling in the state. Proposition 68, backed by non-Indian gambling interests, provided that, unless tribes agreed to a series of stringent conditions contained in the proposal, some racetracks and card clubs would be allowed to operate slot machines. The provisions of Proposition 70, backed by tribal interests, provided for ninety-nine-year compacts with the state, removed limits on the numbers of slot machines in tribal casinos, continued the exclusive right of a tribe to operate casinos, and increased the amount of money contributed by tribes to state funds.[48] Both measures were handily defeated.

SURFING CALIFORNIA: INTERNET RESOURCES

Most local governments have their own Web sites. A good place to start is with the California Land Use Planning Information Network (LUPIN). This site includes links to home pages of counties, cities, councils of governments, and some special districts. See:

http://ceres.ca.gov/planning/lupin_org.html

Links to city and county Web sites are also available from the state home page at *http://www.ca.gov,* while links to school district sites are at

http://www.slocoe.org/resource/calpage1.htm.

Links to ordinances and charters of cities and counties are at:

http://www.igs.berkeley.edu/library/calcodes.html

10. Financing California Government

Everybody wants to go to heaven, but nobody wants to die.

—ANONYMOUS

$\mathcal{M}$ost of us want to "have our cake and eat it too." We demand high levels of service from government but are reluctant to pay for these services with our taxes.

TRADE-OFFS

A Field Poll in December 2001 illustrates the dilemma.[1] In this survey, Californians, by substantial margins, agreed that (1) state and local taxes are either somewhat or much too high, (2) given a choice, it would be better to cut spending than to increase taxes, and (3) spending levels should be maintained or increased in each of ten areas, which together encompass almost all state and local government programs.

At one time, trade-offs between taxing and spending were somewhat easier to make in California than in most other states. At the end of World War II, per capita income was about a third higher than in the country as a whole, and so state and local governments could afford to spend money at relatively high levels without imposing great pain on taxpayers. This advantage steadily eroded, however, and by the early 1990s per capita income in the state was close to the national average.[2]

How choices are made on trade-offs between taxing and spending reflects the basic differences in philosophy between economic liberals and economic conservatives that were introduced in Chapter 3. Liberal and conservative positions differ first of all regarding the overall size of government. Liberals tend to favor a larger government, both in order to provide more opportunities for those who are disadvantaged and as a way of directing investment in economic growth, and they are more willing to raise taxes to pay for government programs. Conservatives tend to favor less government and lower taxes, arguing that investment decisions are best made through the private sector and that people should be able to keep as much of their own money as possible.

Liberals and conservatives differ as well in the kinds of spending that they typically prefer. Liberals favor programs to assist the poor, preserve the environment, and regulate business, while conservatives support programs that promote business and punish criminals. Spending for education is usually popular because it receives strong support from liberals and conservatives as a way both to expand economic opportunities and to invest in a more productive workforce.

Finally, although no politician likes voting for higher taxes, liberals and conservatives differ in the types of taxes they prefer when levies must be imposed. Liberals usually favor taxes that are "progressive," that is, that take a larger proportion from the well-to-do than from the needy. Liberals argue that a progressive tax structure is fairer because it is based on ability to pay. Conservatives tend to oppose progressive taxation, arguing that it punishes people for being successful.

In this chapter, we will examine the patterns and procedures of government finance in California. Keep in mind that budget battles are not at their base over technicalities, but over competing visions of California's future.

OVERVIEW: CALIFORNIA AND OTHER STATES COMPARED

Figure 10.1 shows how state and local government finance in California differs in important respects from what is found in the country as a whole.[3] Numbers for receipts and expenditures are for the 2001–2002 fiscal year, the most recent for which comparative data are available. Included are some categories in which state and local receipts or expenditures in California, when expressed as a proportion of personal income, differ by more than 10 percent from comparable figures for all 50 states taken together.

Compared to other states, California government is much more reliant on personal and corporate income taxes, and less dependent on property taxes. Levies on cars and trucks are also lower, but these (while they can be quite controversial) are relatively minor sources of revenue.

In addition to relying heavily on the income tax, California has one of the country's highest marginal income tax rates. Even before passage of Proposition 63 in November 2004, which added a 1 percent surcharge on incomes over $1,000,000, the state's personal income tax topped out at 9.3 percent for the highest income bracket. The combination has important consequences. Data from the liberal Institute on Taxation and Economic Policy showed that California ranked ninth among the states in progressivity.[4] Looking at tax data from a different perspective, the conservative Tax Foundation ranked California next to last in business climate.[5] Both liberals and conservatives could probably agree that one consequence of California's dependence on income taxes has been considerable volatility in government revenues in recent years. The ups and downs of the stock market, especially in the "dot.com" high tech sector, have had a direct impact on the state budget.[6] Downturns in the market contributed significantly to California's recent budget problems.

FIGURE 10.1
California State and Local Finances, 2001–2002, as Proportion of 2001 Personal Income: Comparison with Data for All States

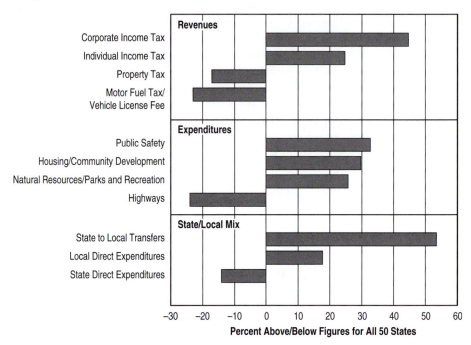

SOURCES: Personal income: *http://www.bea.doc.gov/bea/regional/spi/*; All others: *http://www.census.gov/govs/ www/estimate.html.*

On the expenditure side, California governments spend relatively more than governments in other states on public safety, housing and community development, and natural resources and parks and recreation. On the other hand, California spends relatively less than other states on highways. Other areas of spending are fairly close to the national average. For a number of years, California spent less of its wealth on public education than the norm, but by 2001–2002 it was very near the average. Some of the differences between California and other states are due to the physical characteristics of the state (such as its good weather and abundance of natural resources), while others are the cumulative result of political choices made at various times by various governmental entities.

Public finance in California is more centralized than what is generally found elsewhere. The State of California spends relatively less *directly* than do other states, while local governments in California spend relatively more than their counterparts. This is in large part due to higher levels of fund transfers from the state, which in California account for over two-thirds of state expenditures. These funds have usually come with a number of strings attached, and the resulting heavy involvement of the state in local government activities has been a continuing source of conflict.

BUDGETARY CONSTRAINTS[7]

To a considerable degree, the state budget is beyond the control of either the legislature or the governor. One expert has estimated that only about 15 to 20 percent of the state budget is "controllable."[8] Local governments are even more severely constrained in their fiscal decision making. This is true with regard to both taxes and expenditures.

Tax Constraints

In recent years, voters have approved a number of measures that, in ways large and small, have limited the taxing powers of state and local governments.

The most important of these changes was Proposition 13 (1978). Passage of this measure, also known as the Jarvis-Gann initiative, was a watershed event that, as will be discussed later in this chapter, profoundly altered government finance at both the state and local levels. In the late 1970s, housing values in California were rapidly appreciating. This provided many homeowners with large profits on the investments they had made on their homes. These windfalls, however, were hardly an unmixed blessing. Although increased property values might have made some owners rich (or at least affluent) on paper, this appreciation also meant that as homes were reassessed to reflect their increased market value their property taxes were going up as well. Some people feared that they might literally be taxed out of their homes. Responding to growing discontent and to the apparent inability or unwillingness of elected officials to come to the rescue,[9] Howard Jarvis and his colleague Paul Gann qualified Proposition 13 for the June 1978 ballot. They successfully framed the issue as one pitting homeowners and renters (who pay property taxes indirectly as a cost incorporated into their rents) against wasteful bureaucrats. Campaigning on the slogan, "Save the American Dream" of home ownership, they won a resounding victory. The measure rolled back property taxes to 1975 levels, placed a ceiling of 1 percent of assessed valuation on the rate of property taxation, and provided that, regardless of increased values, property taxes could not go up by more than 2 percent per year, so long as ownership did not change. Proposition 13 also required that increases in state taxes be approved by a two-thirds vote of the total membership of each chamber of the legislature and that new "special" local taxes be approved by two-thirds of the voters. Since 1978, voters have amended Proposition 13 a number of times, but it remains largely intact. Probably the most significant changes have involved financing of school bonds. In 1986, voters approved an amendment exempting from the 1 percent ceiling property taxes needed to repay school facilities bonds if approved by a two-thirds popular vote. In 2000, another measure was approved reducing the required vote to 55 percent.

In the wake of Proposition 13's passage, California changed very quickly from a high-tax state to an average-tax state. In one year, California's state and local tax revenues (as a proportion of personal income) dropped from fourth to twenty-fourth highest in the country.[10]

Proposition 13 has remained popular with voters. By a margin of 53 percent to 30 percent, with the rest undecided, respondents to an April 1998 survey of registered voters by The Field Poll reported that they would vote for the measure if it were on the ballot again. (The initiative actually passed by a margin of 65 percent to 35 percent in 1978.) The proportion of voters who believed that state and local tax levels are "much too high" was almost identical to that found in a 1977 survey. By a two-to-one margin, however, voters agreed that "one of the bad things about Prop. 13 is that most of the funding and control of the public schools has shifted from the local community to the state."[11]

Other initiatives limiting taxes include the following:

- Proposition 6 (1982) largely did away with state inheritance taxes in California. Its passage clearly demonstrates that people do not always vote their self-interest. Even before passage of this measure only a very small percentage of people left estates large enough to be taxable.

- Proposition 7 (1982) permanently "indexed" state income tax rates to inflation. In other words, taxpayers whose incomes have risen no faster than the rate of inflation now do not find themselves paying higher tax rates because of "bracket creep."

- Proposition 62 (1986). This initiative required that increases in general taxes by local governments be submitted to voters for their approval. There was some ambiguity about whether this requirement applied to charter cities.[12]

- Proposition 163 (1992) amended the constitution to repeal a "snack tax" on candy, other snack foods, and bottled water that the legislature had imposed the previous year.

- Proposition 218 (1996) specifically included charter cities in the requirement that general tax increases receive voter approval. It also required that property assessments and property-related fees be submitted to a vote of property owners. Unlike Proposition 13, which at the time of its passage was the focus of great controversy, Proposition 218 attracted relatively little attention during the 1996 general election campaign. It was overshadowed not only by the presidential race but also by several other propositions dealing with campaign finance, affirmative action, the minimum wage, and marijuana. However, it passed by a comfortable margin.

Spending Constraints

Just as lawmakers are limited in the ways in which they can raise money, they are also subject to limitations in the ways they can spend it. For example, in *Serrano v. Priest* (1971), the California Supreme Court ruled that the equal protection clause of the state constitution required that the state provide funding to roughly equalize spending between rich and poor school districts. The court did not specify how this outcome was to be achieved, but its ruling did help set in motion profound changes, to be discussed later, in how public education in California is financed.

In recent years, California voters have approved a number of initiatives and referendums placing restrictions on how money may be spent, including the following:

- Proposition 4 (1979), also known as the Gann initiative (after its chief backer, Paul Gann), was designed to complement Proposition 13 by limiting expenditures as Proposition 13 had limited revenues. The measure provided that revenues exceeding the limit would be rebated to taxpayers. This is just what happened in 1986–1987.[13] Since then, Gann has been severely weakened by other measures (see below).

- Proposition 37 (1984) amended the constitution to allow a state lottery. Selling a vice (gambling) with a virtue (education), it also provided by law that proceeds from the lottery be **earmarked** for educational purposes.

- Proposition 98 (1988) required that a minimum of a little over 40 percent of the state's **general fund** be spent on public school education (K-12 plus community colleges). (A provision was included allowing for temporary suspension of this guarantee by a two-thirds vote of the senate and the assembly, as was done for the 2004–2005 fiscal year.) The measure also provided that a portion of state revenues exceeding Gann limits be allocated to schools rather than returned to taxpayers.

- Propositions 99 (1988) and 10 (1998) raised taxes on tobacco. The first earmarked the resulting revenue for health and for antismoking campaigns, while the second used the money for early childhood development.

- Proposition 111 (1990) relaxed the formula established by the Gann initiative to limit expenditures of state and local governments, and changed the formula created by Proposition 98 for distributing excess revenues to schools and to taxpayers. It also increased gasoline taxes and truck fees and earmarked the revenues for transportation.

- Proposition 172 (1993) earmarked 0.5 percent of the state sales tax for local police, fire, and other public-safety purposes.

- Proposition 42 (2002) provided that, beginning in fiscal year 2008–2009, sales tax revenues from gasoline must be earmarked for transportation.

- Proposition 49 (2002) allocated additional money for before and after school programs.

In November 2004, voters were provided with several additional opportunities to spell out state spending policies. Proposition 1A limited the ability of the legislature to reduce local governments' share of revenues. Proposition 63 called for a tax increase on personal incomes of over $1 million, with the money designated for mental health services. Both passed. Two other measures were defeated. One would have increased telephone taxes, and earmarked the revenue for emergency medical services. Another, like Proposition 1A, would have protected local revenues from the state legislature, but would have gone much further in doing so.

STATE GOVERNMENT FINANCE

The Budget Process[14]

The California fiscal year begins on July 1 and runs to the end of the following June. (The fiscal year for the federal government runs from October 1 to the following September 30.) Long before a fiscal year begins, a lengthy process must be undertaken to put the state budget for that year in place.

As noted in Chapter 7, the governor is responsible for proposing the budget, which must be sent to the legislature by January 10 of each year. The Department of Finance prepares the budget for the governor in much the same way that the federal Office of Management and Budget assists the president. The Governor's Budget, unlike the 13 separate appropriations measures considered by Congress each year at the national level, is treated as a single bill.

Assisting the legislature is the Legislative Analyst's Office, which provides an independent source of expert fiscal information so that the legislature is less dependent on the assumptions made by the executive in preparing the budget. The LAO was established in 1941, more than three decades before the United States Congress set up the Congressional Budget Office to function in a similar capacity in Washington.

During the time that the legislature considers changes to the budget, the governor can play a key role in negotiating with legislative leaders of both parties. (Discussions about budget negotiations often refer to the "Big Five": the governor, the speaker and minority leader of the assembly, and the president pro tem and minority leader of the senate.) More formally, just as action in the legislature typically gains momentum, the governor submits the "May Revision," indicating any alterations made necessary by new conditions in the economy. (At the federal level, the president provides a "mid-session review" in July.[15])

Following passage of the budget, the legislature takes up **trailer bills,** which make any changes to California law that have become necessary as a result of decisions contained in the budget. Although much of this is routine tidying up, provisions of a trailer bill can sometimes become quite controversial in their own right. (Trailer bills function somewhat like the "reconciliation" process at the federal level.[16])

The constitutional deadline for the legislature to pass the budget is June 15, so that the governor can review and sign it before the state fiscal year begins on July 1. In practice, this deadline has often been ignored. In 2002, infighting between Democrats and Republicans in the legislature, and between the legislature and Governor Davis, delayed signing of the budget until September 5, just one day shy of the record for tardiness. Most recently, hopes that the process would be completed before the start of the 2004–2005 fiscal year were dashed, and the budget did not become law until July 31. The difficulty in passing the state budget is in part due to a constitutional requirement that the budget bill must receive the support of at least two-thirds of the membership of both the senate and the assembly. An initiative that would have reduced this requirement to 55 percent was rejected by the voters in March 2004. As a result of the two-thirds requirement, no budget can be passed until a fairly high degree of consensus has been achieved across party lines. As long as it holds at least a third of the seats in either chamber of the legislature (which in recent years it always has), the minority party can maintain substantial influence over the outcome.

Finally, after obtaining approval from the legislature, the budget is sent back to the governor. As noted in Chapter 7, the governor can reduce or eliminate individual "line items" from the budget by using the item veto. The state constitution requires that the budget *proposed* at the beginning of the year by the governor be balanced, that is, that expenditures not exceed revenues. In March 2004, voters approved a referendum (Proposition 58) that also required that the general fund of the budget, as *adopted*, must be balanced.[17] The budget, however, may still contain a hidden deficit if projections of revenues and expenditures turn out to have been overly optimistic. This type of discrepancy is especially likely to occur if the state's economy declines. In addition, debt incurred through the sale of bonds is not included in the balanced budget estimates.

At several points in describing the process, we have noted similarities between the California state budget and that of the federal government. Table 10.1 summarizes some important comparisons.

TABLE 10.1
The Federal and California Budget Processes

	California	Federal
Executive Proposes Budget	January	February
Executive Assisted by	Department of Finance	Office of Management and Budget
Revision by Executive	May	July
Legislature Approves Budget, Assisted by	Legislative Analyst's Office	Congressional Budget Office
Number of Appropriations Bills (Excluding Supplemental Appropriations)	1	13
Needed to Pass	Two-thirds Majority of Total Membership in Each Chamber	Simple Majority of Members Present and Voting in Each Chamber
Required Adjustments to Law Accomplished Through	Trailer Bills	Reconciliation
Item Veto	Yes	No
Fiscal Year Begins	July 1	October 1

Where the Money Comes From, and Where it Goes

State funds fall into several categories, as shown in Figure 10.2.[18]

- *The general fund.* These revenues are relatively free of constraints on how they can be spent, but there are still major limitations, most notably those imposed by Proposition 98. By one estimate, two-thirds or more of even the general fund is earmarked.[19]

- *Special funds.* These revenues are set aside for specific purposes. The distinction between the general fund and **special funds** is not a clear one, not only because of strings attached to the general fund, but also because money is sometimes transferred from one type of fund to another, often for political purposes.

- *Bond funds.* These are earmarked, usually for long-term projects such as new buildings.

- *Federal funds.* These also come with conditions on how they can be spent. This is especially true for "categorical grants," while "block grants" allow more flexibility.

- *Nongovernmental cost funds.* These consist of various accounts (such as pension funds) that are held by the state and included for information purposes in a listing of total state funds.

Figure 10.3 shows the estimated general and special fund revenues and expenditures for the 2003–2004 fiscal year.[20] (Federal and nongovernmental cost funds are excluded because they are not usually considered part of the state budget. Bond funds are excluded

---

FIGURE 10.2
Total State Spending Plan, Estimates for
2003–2004 (in $1,000s)

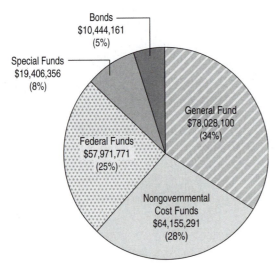

SOURCE: Department of Finance.

because they fluctuate a great deal from year to year and because they cannot really be identified with the budget for any one year—a bond may be approved in one fiscal year, spent in others, and paid off over decades. A little under half of all federal funds are for health and human services. Bond fund expenditures in 2003–2004 were mostly for K–12 education, natural resources, and higher education.)

At the beginning of this chapter, we noted that California relies more than most states on personal income taxes. Figure 10.3 shows that, in absolute terms, it is the largest

---

FIGURE 10.3
General Fund Receipts and Expenditures, Estimates for 2003–2004 (in $1,000s)

REVENUES

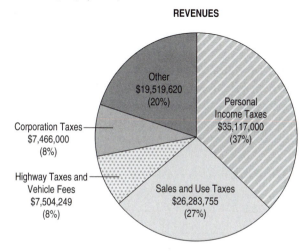

EXPENDITURES

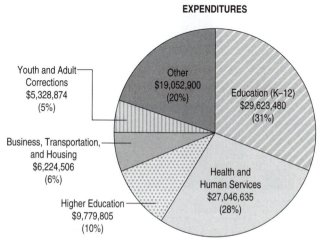

SOURCE: California Department of Finance.

source of revenue for the state. Sales and use taxes are the second largest revenue source, and together with the personal income tax make up almost two-thirds of state revenue. To a lesser degree, corporation taxes and taxes and fees on transportation are also significant sources of state revenue.

K–12 education was easily the biggest expenditure category, accounting for almost a third of state spending (the bulk of it transferred to local school districts). Health and human services (much of it actually spent by county governments) makes up over a quarter of spending.

LOCAL GOVERNMENT FINANCE

General-Purpose Governments

In Chapter 9, we saw that cities are primarily involved in providing physical services to residents, that counties have a larger role in the provision of social services (especially health and welfare), and that both play important parts in public safety. Cities and counties also differ in where they get their money. As shown in Figure 10.4,[21] counties are now heavily dependent on other levels of government. In 2001–2002, the latest year for which information was available, counties received about 64 percent of their money from

FIGURE 10.4
Sources of City and County Revenues, 2001–2002

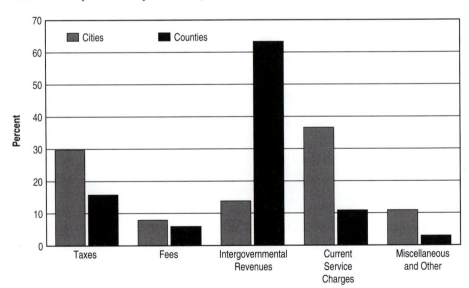

SOURCE: California State Controller.

"intergovernmental revenues" (about two-thirds of that from the state and a third from the federal government). That same year, cities depended on intergovernmental revenues for only about 14 percent of their funds, raising much more of their own money from a combination of service charges (mostly for utilities and waste disposal) and taxes.[22]

Special-Purpose Governments

It is difficult to generalize about California's many special districts, except to note that most of their revenue comes from "enterprise activities," such as provision of water, utilities, and transit.[23] When it comes to school districts, they, like counties, are heavily dependent on other levels of government for funding, receiving most of their revenues from the state (54.5 percent of total revenues) and federal (8.2 percent) governments.[24]

SURFING CALIFORNIA: INTERNET RESOURCES

The governor's perspective on the budget is provided by the Department of Finance. Visit its Web site at:

http://www.dof.ca.gov

The legislative analyst's critique of the governor's budget may be found at:

http://www.lao.ca.gov

The California Taxpayers' Association analyzes California budget issues from a conservative perspective at:

http://caltax.org

The California Budget Project does the same from a liberal point of view at:

http://www.cbp.org

Glossary

Absentee voting. Voting by sending in one's ballot rather than by going in person to one's local precinct.

American Independent Party. A party founded in 1967 by followers of segregationist candidate George Wallace; conservative on both social and economic issues.

Assembly. The "lower" chamber of the California state legislature.

At-large districts. Districts in which all candidates run throughout the entire jurisdiction of a decision-making body (such as a city council or school board).

Attorney general. A statewide elected official; the state's chief law enforcement officer; head of the California Department of Justice.

Board of Equalization. A five-member board consisting of the controller and four other members chosen from single-member districts; collects various taxes, including the sales tax; exercises general supervision over county assessors.

Blanket primary. A primary in which a voter can vote for any candidate for any office, without regard to party. The candidate receiving the most votes within a party becomes the nominee of that party.

Charter. A governing document allowing a city or county more flexibility than would be the case under the state's general law.

Civil law. Law governing relations between persons (including artificial persons such as businesses and even the government). In a civil law suit, the dispute is between two persons or set of persons, one of whom claims to have been harmed by the other.

Civil service system. One in which government employees are chosen through competitive examinations or other merit-based criteria.

Closed primary. A primary in which a voter must choose from candidates within the party with which the voter is registered.

Communitarians. Communitarians favor an activist government and are generally liberal on economic issues and conservative on social issues. Also called "populists."

Compulsory referendum. A matter that must be referred to the voters for approval, including constitutional amendments, creation or amendment of a local government charter, and general obligation bonds.

Conference committee. A committee appointed to reconcile differences between assembly and senate versions of a bill.

Conservatives. Conservatives favor market-based approaches to economic problems and generally support government action to maintain social order.

Contract cities. Cities that arrange for various services (usually including police and fire protection) to be provided by the county or other outside agencies, rather than provide such services themselves.

Controller. A statewide elected official; responsible for disbursement of state funds; serves on the state Board of Equalization.

Courts of Appeal. Intermediate level courts that hear appeals from trial court verdicts.

Criminal law. Law designed to protect the public order. In a criminal case, the defendant is alleged to have done harm to the people as a whole by violating this order.

Cross-filing. A system (abolished in the 1950s) that allowed a candidate to run in the primaries of more than one party.

Department of Finance. An agency that assists the governor in fiscal matters, most importantly in the preparation of the state budget.

Direct democracy. Decision making by the voters themselves rather than through representatives. The initiative is the purest form of direct democracy, though the term also includes the referendum and the recall.

Earmarking. Setting aside certain sources of revenue for specific purposes. Gasoline taxes, for example, are "earmarked" for the transportation budget.

Federal. Referring to a form of government in which both the central government and regional governments enjoy independent powers.

Field Poll, The. A survey by The Field Institute, a San Francisco-based research firm.

General election. An election held on the first Tuesday after the first Monday in November of even-numbered years. Federal, state, and some local offices are contested at this time. Initiatives and referendums also appear on the general election ballot.

General fund. The primary source of revenue for the state budget. It is subject to fewer restrictions than "special funds" or funds from the federal government. Constraints do exist, most notably the requirement that a little over 40 percent of general fund revenues normally must be spent for education (kindergarten through community college).

General law. State law that applies to cities and counties that do not have their own charters.

Gerrymander. A legislative redistricting plan drawn up in such a way as to favor one party or interest over others.

Governor. A statewide elected official; the state's chief executive.

Grand jury. A body of citizens at the county level that can issue indictments in criminal cases and that has a "watchdog" role over local government.

Green Party. Qualifying for the ballot in 1992, the Green Party is liberal on both social and economic issues, with a special emphasis on environmental activism.

Indictment. A decision by a grand jury that sufficient evidence exists to warrant a criminal trial.

Initiative. A proposition placed on the ballot through voter petition.

Insurance commissioner. A statewide elected official; head of the California Department of Insurance.

Item veto. An action by the governor to reduce or eliminate an appropriation item in the budget. Like other gubernatorial vetoes, it can be overridden by a two-thirds vote of the membership of the assembly and of the senate.

Judicial Council. A body charged with general administration and oversight of the state's courts.

Legislative Analyst's Office. An agency that assists the legislature in fiscal matters, most importantly in the analysis of the state budget.

Liberals. Liberals support government action to reduce economic inequality and generally seek to limit the role of government in maintaining social order.

Libertarian Party. Founded in 1971, the Libertarian Party is, as its name implies, economically conservative and socially liberal on most issues.

Libertarians. Libertarians are those who favor very limited government. This stance results in conservative positions on most economic matters and liberal positions on most social issues (gun control being a notable exception).

Lieutenant governor. A statewide elected official whose duties include presiding over the state senate, serving as acting governor when the governor is out of state or temporarily unable to serve, and becoming governor if that office becomes vacant.

Local Agency Formation Commission (LAFCO). An agency, located in each county, charged with coordinating changes in local government organization, such as incorporations and annexations.

Natural Law Party. Followers of the Maharishi Mahesh Yogi founded the Natural Law Party. It qualified for the ballot in California in 1995.

Nonpartisan. Without regard to party. In California, all local elected offices, all judicial offices, and the Superintendent of Public Instruction are chosen on a nonpartisan basis.

Office-bloc ballot. A ballot form used in California and some other states, in which candidates are grouped by office rather than by party. This type of ballot tends to discourage straight-ticket voting for one party.

Open primary. A primary that allows the voter to select the ballot of any party, whether he or she is registered with that party or not, but the voter is then limited to candidates from within that party in all partisan contests.

Partisan. With regard to party. Contests among candidates who have been nominated for office in their parties' primaries.

Party-column ballot. A ballot form used in some states but not in California, in which candidates are grouped by party as well as by office. This type of ballot tends to encourage straight-ticket voting for one party.

Peace and Freedom Party. Growing out of the "New Left" movement of the 1960s, the Peace and Freedom Party first qualified for the ballot in 1967. The party "is committed to socialism, democracy, ecology, feminism and racial equality."

Petit jury. The trial jury in a civil or criminal case.

Petition referendum. A procedure in which citizens petition to override a measure approved by the legislature by placing it on the ballot for voter approval.

Plural executive. An executive branch with two or more elected persons, each with his or her own independent mandate and powers. Whereas the president of the United States is *the* chief executive of the federal government, California and all other states have plural executives.

President pro tempore (or president pro tem). In the senate, the "president for the time" or acting presiding officer (in the absence of the lieutenant governor). The power of this office derives primarily from the fact that the president pro tem chairs the powerful senate Rules Committee.

Primary. Held in the spring of even-numbered years, the primary (that is, first) election is used to narrow down the candidates for election to an office. Ballot propositions also appear on the primary ballot.

Progressives. Supporters of a movement that flourished at the start of the twentieth century. Distrustful of political parties and the state legislature, the Progressives advocated direct democracy. They deserve much of the credit or blame for many of the distinctive features of California politics.

Proposition. A measure placed on the ballot through initiative or referendum.

Ranked choice voting. Also known as preference or single transferable voting. Voters rank candidates in order of preference. If a voter's choice of candidates is eliminated, that person's vote is then transferred to his or her second and subsequent choices until one candidate has received a majority.

Recall. An election to remove an official from office before the end of his or her term.

Redistricting. The drawing of electoral boundary lines. Redistricting is normally required after each decennial U.S. Census to ensure that each district has about the same population.

Referendum. A ballot proposition that is referred to the voters for approval by a legislative body.

Reform Party. Founded by followers of Ross Perot, the Reform Party qualified for the California ballot in 1995, but was disqualified after the 2002 elections.

Representative democracy. Decision making through elected representatives.

Secretary of state. A statewide elected official; the state's chief elections officer.

Senate. The "upper" chamber of the California state legislature.

Single-member districts. Districts created when a decision-making body (such as a city council or school board) is divided into geographic sub-areas, with each area electing one member.

Speaker. The presiding officer of the assembly.

Special district. A unit of local government with jurisdiction limited to one or more specific functions (water distribution, fire control, redevelopment, etc.).

Special election. An election held to fill a vacant office or to recall an incumbent. Also sometimes used for votes on propositions.

Special funds. Revenue set aside for a specific purpose, such as education or transportation.

Standing committee. A permanent committee of either the assembly or the senate. Major legislation must usually be referred to one or more standing committees in each chamber before being considered by the full chamber.

Superintendent of public instruction. A statewide elected official, the only such chosen in a nonpartisan election; director of the California Department of Education and executive officer of the state Board of Education.

Superior courts. California's trial courts.

Supreme Court. The state's highest court or court of last resort.

Trailer bills. Bills taken up following approval of the state budget in order to bring state law into conformity with the budget.

Treasurer. A statewide elected official; California's chief investment officer.

Unitary. Referring to a form of government in which regional sub-units have only those powers granted by the central government.

A Note on Sources

Increasingly, sources originally intended as hard copy are also available online, and often are more accessible in this form. For all sources that are found exclusively on the Internet, I have provided the address, or "Uniform Resource Locator" (URL), and the date of access. In most other cases, I have not provided the URL, but instead offer the following general guidelines.

Online sources are normally available as "html" (for "hypertext markup language") or "pdf" (for "portable document format") files, or both. To read pdf files, your computer must have Adobe Acrobat Reader, which can be downloaded at no charge from Adobe at *http://www.adobe.com/products/acrobat/readstep.html*.

Many publications of the U.S. Bureau of the Census (including the *Statistical Abstract of the United States*) are available online at *http://www.census.gov*.

The California Constitution is available online at *http://www.leginfo.ca.gov/const.html*.

The California Code, a compilation of the state's laws, is at *http://www.leginfo.ca.gov/calaw.html,* although I have found that, unless I knew very specifically what I was looking for, it was often easier to consult the hard copy version by West Publishing Company. The Hastings Law Library maintains a comprehensive and searchable "California Ballot Propositions Database" at *http://library.uchastings.edu/library/Research%20Databases/*.

Recent decisions of the California Supreme Court and some appellate court decisions are at *http://www.courtinfo.ca.gov*, as are publications of the Judicial Council, including the *Court Statistics Report*. See also "California Case Law: 1934–Present," at *http://www.findlaw.com/cacases/index.html* (free registration required).

For United States Supreme Court decisions, visit *http://fedbbs.access.gpo.gov/court01.htm* or *http://guide.lp.findlaw.com/casecode/supreme.html*. See also the comment below on Lexis-Nexis Academic Universe.

The full text of E. Dotson Wilson and Brian S. Ebbert's *California's Legislature* is available at *http://www.leginfo.ca.gov/califleg.html*.

Most publications of executive agencies cited in the text are available online. These include those of the Secretary of State (*http://www.ss.ca.gov*), the Department of Finance (*http://www.dof.ca.gov/*), and the State Controller (*http://www.sco.ca.gov*). Other state publications include those of the California Research Bureau (*http://www.library.ca.gov/html/statseg2a.cfm*).

A number of private organizations provide many of their publications online, including the Public Policy Institute of California (*http://www.ppic.org*), the Institute on Taxation and Economic Policy (*http://www.itepnet.org*), and the Tax Foundation (*http://www.taxfoundation.org*).

The Field Poll's press releases and *California Opinion Index* are online at *http://field.com/fieldpollonline/subscribers/*.

Almost all newspapers publish online versions. Many charge a small fee for the full text of articles from their archives (but see Lexis-Nexis Academic Universe, below).

Some online sites are accessible only on a subscription basis. Fortunately, there is a good chance that your campus has a license for some or all of these. Contact a reference librarian on your campus, or visit your campus library Web site.

One very useful subscription service is Lexis-Nexis Academic Universe. Under "News," check "General News" for articles in major national newspapers and magazines, including the *Los Angeles Times,* and check "U.S. News" for articles in state newspapers and magazines, including the *California Journal.* Look in "Legal Research" for state and federal court decisions.

J-STOR (short for "journal storage") is a subscription service that contains the full text of many articles in scholarly journals.

Notes

1. "America, Only More So"

1. Often attributed to novelist and essayist Wallace Stegner, the phrase "America, only more so" was used to describe California at least as early as 1883. See "Current Comment," *Overland Monthly* (December 1883), 658.
2. Quoted in Carl Nolte, "California Century, Part Seven: Now: Change at the Speed of Light," *San Francisco Chronicle*, 30 May 1999.
3. "Living in California," *California Opinion Index* (January 2001): 3.
4. Michael Barone and Grant Ujifusa, *The Almanac of American Politics 2000* (Washington, D.C.: National Journal, 1999), 154ff.
5. Fred Barnes, "California Doesn't Matter: The Political Future Once Happened There; No More," *The Weekly Standard*, 31 July 2000.
6. Peter Schrag, "Politics 2000: Has California Become Irrelevant?" *Sacramento Bee*, 7 August 2000.
7. These statistics are from Kathleen O'Leary Morgan and Scott Morgan, *State Rankings 2004* (Lexington, Ky.: Morgan Quitno, 2004), 32, 405, 554.
8. Deborah Reed, *California's Rising Income Inequality: Causes and Concerns* (San Francisco: Public Policy Institute of California, 1999), 1.
9. U.S. Census Bureau, "Gini Ratios by State," (8 July 2004) *http://www.census.gov/hhes/income/histinc/state/state4.html* (accessed 7 November 2004). California fared even worse when family income was used as the measure, finishing second in inequality.
10. U.S. Census Bureau, "Ranking Tables 2002," *American Community Survey*, (1 September 2003) *http://www.census.gov/acs/www/Products/Ranking/2002/R08T040.htm* (accessed 7 November 2004).
11. Martin Kasindorf, "In Central Valley, a Different California," *USA Today*, 17 December 1998; John Ritter, "Priced Out of Silicon Valley: Insane Housing Market Is Pushing Away Teachers, Police," *USA Today*, 18 May 2000.
12. This includes the nonpartisan office of superintendent of public instruction, held by Jack O'Connell, a Democrat.
13. Donald B. Dodd, *Historical Statistics of the States of the United States: Two Centuries of the Census, 1790–1990* (Westport, Conn.: Greenwood Press, 1993), 10–11.
14. U.S. Census Bureau, "Ranking Tables 2002."
15. California Department of Finance, "Population Projections by Race/Ethnicity, Gender and Age for California and Its Counties 2000–2050," (May 2004)

http://www.dof.ca.gov/HTML/DEMOGRAP/DRU_Publications/Projections/P3/ CALIFORNIA%20.XLS (accessed 7 November 2004).

16. *Ibid.*

17. Hans P. Johnson, *How Many Californians? A Review of Population Projections for the State* (San Francisco: Public Policy Institute of California, 1999).

18. Bruce Cain and Roderick Kiewiet, "California's Coming Minority Majority," *Public Opinion* 9 (February/March 1986): 50–52.

2. The State Constitution

1. Robert Weissberg, *Understanding American Government*, 2nd ed. (New York: Random House, 1986), 35.

2. George Skelton, "In This Poker Game, the Indians Hold the Best Hand," *Los Angeles Times*, 30 August 1999.

3. California Senate, *The Constitutions of California and of the United States, with Related Documents*, 2003–2004 ed. (Sacramento: State of California, 2003).

4. California Constitution, art. X B, sect. 6.

5. For the text of the Constitution of 1849, see California Secretary of State, "California State Archives: Records of the Constitutional Convention of 1849," *http://www.ss.ca.gov/archives/level3_const1849.html* (accessed 24 October 2004).

6. E. Dotson Wilson and Brian S. Ebbert, *California's Legislature* (Sacramento: California State Assembly, 2000), 9.

7. *Ibid.*, 10. Constitutional amendments had to be approved by a majority vote of two successive legislatures and then approved by a majority of those qualified to vote for the state legislature.

8. Carl Brent Swisher, *Motivation and Political Technique in the California Constitutional Convention, 1878–79* (New York: Da Capo Press, 1969 [1930]), 17.

9. *Ibid.*, 9.

10. James Bryce, *The American Commonwealth*, rev. ed., vol. 2 (New York: Macmillan, 1928 [1914]), 431.

11. Swisher, *Motivation and Political Technique, passim.*

12. Hyung-chan Kim, *A Legal History of Asian Americans, 1790–1990* (Westport, Conn.: Greenwood Press, 1994), 56–57.

13. Swisher, *Motivation and Political Technique, passim.*

14. Wilson and Ebbert, *California's Legislature*, 11.

15. George Mowry, *The California Progressives* (Berkeley: University of California Press, 1951).

16. California Constitution, art. II, sect. 8; art. XVIII, sect. 3.

17. National Conference of State Legislatures, "Initiative, Referendum and Recall," (2004) *http://www.ncsl.org/programs/legman/elect/initiat.htm* (accessed 24 October 2004). Some of these states provide the initiative only for statutes or only for constitutional amendments, and some provide for only an indirect initiative in which measures, after having acquired the requisite number of signatures, are submitted to the

legislature and appear on the ballot only if they fail to win legislative approval. In California, the indirect initiative was discontinued at the state level in 1966.

18. California Constitution, art. II sect. 9; art. XVIII, sect. 1.

19. For a list of petition referendums through 1993, see *A Study of California Budget Measures 1884–1993* (Sacramento: Secretary of State, 1994).

20. California Constitution, art. II, sect. 10.

21. National Conference of State Legislatures, "Initiative, Referendum and Recall."

22. The all-time record for a single election was set during the Progressive Era in 1914, when forty-eight statewide measures appeared on the general election ballot. Since 1960, when ballot propositions were regularly a part of the primary as well as the general election ballot, the high-water mark was attained in November 1988, when voters had to wade through twenty-nine propositions statewide. See *A Study of California Ballot Measures 1884–1993*, 2–3.

23. California Constitution, art. II, sect. 14, and California Election Code, sects. 11000 *et seq.*

24. National Conference of State Legislatures, "Initiative, Referendum and Recall." Judges are the officeholders most commonly exempted from recall procedures. See *The Book of the States, 2004* (Lexington, Ky.: Council of State Governments, 2004), 316–318.

25. California Constitution, art. IV, sect. 18.

26. California Secretary of State, "California Recall History," (7 October 2003) *http://www. ss.ca.gov/elections/sov/2003_special/contests.pdf* (accessed 24 October 2004).

27. Mark DiCamillo and Mervin Field, "Increased Majority of Voters (58%) Ready to Recall Davis. Governor's Job Ratings Decline to Lowest Level Yet. Voters Divided Over Whether Davis Should Resign or Fight the Recall." *The Field Poll*, Press release #2081, 15 August 2003.

28. California Secretary of State, "Statement of Vote, 2003 Statewide Special Election, October 7, 2003" (14 November 2003).

29. *Los Angeles Times,* "Times' Exit Poll Results," 28 October 2003 *http://images. latimes.com/media/acrobat/2003-10/10000373.pdf* (accessed 24 October 2004); *Washington Post,* "California Recall Election Exit Poll—October 7, 2003,"(2003) *http://www.washingtonpost.com/wp-srv/politics/replacementballotexitpoll.html* (accessed 24 October 2004).

30. California Constitution, art. XVIII.

31. *Ibid.*, art. II, sect. 8, and art. XVIII, sects. 1, 3.

32. Claire Cooper, "Courts Often the Last Stop in Ballot Measure Process," *Sacramento Bee*, 6 August 1996.

33. *Senate v. Jones,* 21 Cal. 4th 1142 (1999). The only precedents cited by the court for its decision were two appellate court rulings. Whether this case will turn out to be an exception or whether it signals a new course by the court remains to be seen.

34. California Constitution, art. XVIII, sect. 1.

35. *Californians for an Open Primary v. Shelley*, (30 July 2004) *http://www.courtinfo. ca.gov/opinions/documents/C047231.PDF* (accessed 24 October 2004).

36. *The Book of the States, 2004,* 10–11. Technically, the Alabama constitution has been amended more often, but most of these are local amendments that do not impact the state as a whole.
37. Max Vanzi, "Legislature OKs Bill Easing Charter School Expansion," *Los Angeles Times,* 1 May 1998; Broder, *Democracy Derailed,* 171–173.
38. *Ibid.,* 106–109.
39. "Initiatives: The Monster That Threatens California Politics," *Los Angeles Times,* 12 November 1990; see also Peter Schrag, "California, Here We Come," *Atlantic Monthly,* March 1998, 20, 22, 30–31.
40. Author's analysis of first October 1990 Field Poll.
41. David Broder, *Democracy Derailed: Initiative Campaigns and the Power of Money* (New York: Harcourt, 2000), 1.
42. California Secretary of State, "November 3, 1998 General Election: Financing California's Statewide Ballot Measures: Campaign Receipts and Expenditures Through December 31, 1998," *http://www.ss.ca.gov/prd/bmprimary98_final/bmprimary98_final_mainpage.htm* (accessed 24 October 2004). Expensive battles over ballot propositions are not a new phenomenon. In 1922, a total of over $1 million was spent on the measures on that year's ballot, an amount equivalent to around $10 million in today's dollars. See David McCuan, Shaun Bowler, Todd Donovan, and Ken Fernandez, "California's Political Warriors: Campaign Professionals and the Initiative Process," in Shaun Bowler, Todd Donovan, and Caroline J. Tolbert, eds., *Citizens as Legislators: Direct Democracy in the United States* (Columbus: Ohio State University Press, 1998), 57–58.
43. Elizabeth R. Gerber, *Interest Group Influence in the California Initiative Process* (San Francisco: Public Policy Institute of California, 1998).
44. Claire Cooper, "Courts Often the Last Stop"; Peter Schrag, "The Initiative, the Courts and the Crocodile in the Bathtub," *Sacramento Bee,* 5 July 2000.
45. Broder, *Democracy Derailed,* 85.
46. "A Digest on How California Voters View Statewide Ballot Proposition Elections," *California Opinion Index* (October 1997). The wording of the question referred to "ballot propositions" and did not distinguish between initiatives and referendums.
47. "Legislation by Initiative vs. Through Elected Representatives," *California Opinion Index,* November 1999.
48. The descriptions that follow are based on Charlene Wear Simmons, *California's Statewide Initiative Process* (Sacramento: California Research Bureau, 1997), 17–23.

3. Public Opinion and the Media

1. Quoted in Elizabeth Kolbert, "Campaign in California: Little but Commercials," *New York Times,* 22 May 1992, as cited in Roger R. Davidson and William J. Oleszek, *Congress and Its Members,* 7th ed. (Washington, D.C.: Congressional Quarterly Press, 2000), 89.
2. Kenneth Janda, Jeffrey M. Berry, and Jerry Goldman, *The Challenge of Democracy,* 8th ed. (Boston: Houghton Mifflin, 2005), Chapter 1.

3. Analysis provided to the author by Professor Hout. His data are from the General Social Surveys conducted by the National Opinion Research Center.

4. John R. Owens, Edmund Costantini, and Louis F. Weschler, *California Politics and Parties* (New York: Macmillan, 1970), 125–132; Michael Paul Rogin and John L. Shover, *Political Change in California: Critical Elections and Social Movements, 1890–1966* (Westport, Conn.: Greenwood Press, 1970), 153–212; Raymond E. Wolfinger and Fred Greenstein, "Comparing Political Regions: The Case of California," *American Political Science Review* 63 (March 1969): 74–85. But see, for example, Phillip L. Gianos, "Two Californias or One: Political Culture and Community Public Policy," in Robert S. Ross, ed., *Perspectives on Local Government in California* (Belmont, Calif.: Star Publishing, 1987), 2–3.

5. Rogin and Shover, *Political Change in California*, 183.

6. Secretary of State, "Election Results and Dates," (n.d.) *http://www.ss.ca.gov/elections/elections.htm* (accessed 5 November 2004); Nancy Wride and Amanda Covarrubias, "Tally Ho! A Bush-Kerry Tie Is Unknotted," *Los Angeles Times*, 4 November 2004.

7. Jenifer Warren, "Rural Voter Bid to Divide State Seen as Quixotic Cause," *Los Angeles Times*, 4 June 1992. In the combined tally for all thirty-one counties participating, 53 percent of those voting favored the measure to separate. Source: *Statement of Vote, June 1992* (Sacramento: Secretary of State, 1992).

8. "Large Majority (60 percent) Against Splitting State in Two, 79 Percent Disapprove of Three-Way Division," *The Field Poll*, press release # 1692, 2 November 1993.

9. Derived from data in *Los Angeles Times Poll* (2004) *http://www.latimes.com/news/custom/timespoll/* (accessed 6 November 2004). Results for all respondents were estimated by taking a weighted average of male and female respondents.

10. Bruce Cain and Rodrick Kiewiet, "California's Coming Minority Majority," *Public Opinion* 9 (February/March 1986): 50–52.

11. Thad L. Beyle, *State Government: CQ's Guide to Current Issues and Activities 1997–98* (Washington, D.C.: Congressional Quarterly Press, 1997), 58.

12. Greg Krikorian, "Senate Race Is a Sleeping Giant—So Far," *Los Angeles Times*, 18 January 2000; Edward L. Lascher, Jr., "Press Coverage of Propositions Is Sparse in California," *Public Affairs Report*, March 1997, 9–10.

13. Howard Rosenberg, "California News Without a Car Chase in Sight," *Los Angeles Times*, 7 June 2002.

14. Tracy Weston and Beth Givens, *The California Channel: A New Public Affairs Television Network for the State* (Los Angeles: Center for Responsive Government, 1989), 45–64.

15. Alan Greenblatt, "Strong Governor," *Governing*, July 2004, 24.

16. Charles Layton and Jennifer Dorroh, "The State of the American Newspaper: Resurrection in Dixie," *American Journalism Review* 25 (June/July 2003), 49.

17. "Political Parties and the Party System," *California Opinion Index* (April 1999). See also John Jacobs, "Except for Schools, State's Voters Are Disengaged," *Sacramento Bee*, 9 September 1999.

4. Political Parties and Interest Groups

1. Assemblyman X as told to Lester Velie, "This Is How Payola Works in Politics," *Reader's Digest,* August 1960, 50. "Assemblyman X" was later identified as Unruh. See Lou Cannon, *Ronnie and Jesse: A Political Odyssey* (Garden City, N.Y.: Doubleday, 1969), 104–105.

2. Michael J. Ross, *California: Its Government and Politics,* 5th ed. (Belmont, Calif.: Wadsworth, 1996), 66.

3. "Who's Liberal; Who's Conservative," *California Journal,* March 1991, 138–140.

4. The distinctions made in this section among the "party organization," the "party in the electorate," and the "party in government" are from Frank Sorauf, *Political Parties in America* (Boston: Little, Brown, 1968), 10–11.

5. For a more detailed discussion, see John R. Owens, Edmund Costantini, and Louis E. Weschler, *California Politics and Parties* (New York: Macmillan, 1970), 2–16.

6. *The Book of the States, 2004* (Lexington, Ky.: Council of State Governments, 2004), 271–272.

7. *Eu v. San Francisco County Democratic Central Committee,* 489 U.S. 214 (1989).

8. "Ban on Party Endorsements for Judges Ruled Unconstitutional," *Los Angeles Times,* 8 February 1998; American Judicature Society, "Judicial Campaigns and Elections," *http://www.ajs.org/js/CA_elections.htm* (accessed 6 November 2004).

9. For a discussion of the 1990 gubernatorial primary campaign, see Gerald C. Lubenow, ed., *California Votes: The 1990 Governor's Race* (Berkeley, Calif.: Institute of Governmental Studies, 1991), 107–152, especially 112.

10. Bill Stall and Cathleen Decker, "Brown Focuses on Economy to Boost Campaign," *Los Angeles Times,* 30 April 1994.

11. *California Democratic Party v. Jones* 530 U.S.567 (2000).

12. The terminology is a little confusing. The official title for Proposition 198 as it appeared on the March 1996 ballot referred to it as an "open" rather than as a "blanket" primary. Justice Scalia's decision, referring to Proposition 198 as a blanket primary, follows the language normally used by political scientists.

13. "Bylaws of the California Republican Party," *California Republican Party,* (23 February 2003) *http://www.cagop.org/about/bylaws.pdf* (accessed 6 November 2004).

14. "California Democratic Party State Central Committee By-Laws," *California Democratic Party,* (December 2000) *http://www.kintera.org/atf/cf/{CCC02147-2FC6-45A1-96FD-C95D72F7D4B2}/ByLawsAndRules.pdf* (accessed 6 November 2004).

15. Charles G. Bell and Charles M. Price, *California Government Today,* 4th ed. (Pacific Grove, Calif.: Brooks/Cole, 1992), 142.

16. *California Official Voter Information Guide* (Sacramento: Secretary of State, 2000), 13–14, 54ff.

17. Hugo Martin, "Division Stalls Democrats in San Bernardino," *Los Angeles Times,* 8 May 2003; George Skelton, "Bad News for Democrats: GOP Pipes Down on Social Issues," *Los Angeles Times,* 18 September 2003.

18. Alan Greenblatt, "The Soft-Money Crackdown," *Governing*, March 2004, 34–39.

19. Derived from data in *Los Angeles Times Poll* (2004) *http://www.latimes.com/news/custom/timespoll/* (accessed 6 November 2004). These are the same measures as those analyzed in Chapter 3, with the addition of two more for which the *Times* did not provide comparable breakdowns by ethnicity, but did provide partisan breakdowns.

20. The requirements for qualifying a party for the ballot are spelled out in California Secretary of State, "Political Party Qualification," (2000) *http://www.ss.ca.gov/elections/elections_t.htm* (accessed 6 November 2004).

21. Lester Velie, "The Secret Boss of California, Part One," *Collier's,* 13 August 1949, 11–13, 71–73; Lester Velie, "The Secret Boss of California, Part Two," *Collier's,* 20 August 1949, 12–13, 60, 62–64.

22. Arthur H. Samish and Bob Thomas, *The Secret Boss of California: The Life and High Times of Art Samish* (New York: Crown, 1971).

23. Clive S. Thomas and Ronald J. Hrebenar, "Interest Group Power in the Fifty States: Trends Since the Late 1970s," *Comparative State Politics* 20 (August 1999): 13.

24. Statistics on lobbying receipts and expenditures were taken from California Secretary of State, "Cal-Access: California Automated Lobbying and Campaign Contribution & Expenditure Search System" (24 August 2004) *http://dbsearch.ss.ca.gov/* (accessed 24 August 2004).

25. John Fund, "Richie and Cruz," *Wall Street Journal*, 12 September 2003.

26. Robert Salladay and Christian Berthelsen, "Lobbyist's Outbursts Spur Calls for Reform," *San Francisco Chronicle*, 10 June 2003.

27. *California Ballot Pamphlet, General Election, November 6, 1992* (Sacramento: Secretary of State), 69.

28. Rich Jones, "NCSL Studies the Effects of Term Limits," *State Legislatures Magazine,* (December 1999) *http://www.ncsl.org/programs/pubs/1299mich.htm#NCSL* (accessed 6 November 2004).

5. Campaigns and Elections

1. *Bowling Alone: The Collapse and Renewal of American Community* (New York: Simon and Schuster, 2000), 341.

2. Fox News, "2004 Democrat Delegate Vote Allocation by Primary or Caucus Date," *http://www.foxnews.com/projects/pdf/2004demdel_allocation.pdf* (accessed 6 November 2004).

3. CNN, "Primary Results: California—March 2" (12 March 2004) *http://www.cnn.com/ELECTION/2004/primaries/pages/states/CA/index.html* (accessed 6 November 2004).

4. *California Election Code*, sect. 10700.

5. *http://www.ss.ca.gov/elections/votereg1.html* (accessed 6 November 2004).

6. U.S. Department of Justice, Civil Rights Division, Voting Section, "About Language Minority Voting Rights," (9 February 2004) *http://www.usdoj.gov/crt/voting/sec_203/activ_203.htm* (accessed 6 November 2004).

7. Secretary of State, "Decertification and Withdrawal of Approval of Certain DRE Voting Systems and Conditional Approval of the Use of Certain DRE Voting Systems," 30 April 2004, *http://www.ss.ca.gov/elections/ks_dre_papers/decert1.pdf* (accessed 6 November 2004); Stuart Pfeifer, "State Blocks Digital Voting," *Los Angeles Times*, 1 May 2004; "Paper or Machine? E-voting Is Coming—If Problems Are Resolved," (editorial) *San Diego Union Tribune*, 15 June 2004.

8. City and County of San Francisco Department of Elections, "Ranked-Choice Voting," (2004) *http://www.sfgov.org/site/election_page.asp?id=24269* (accessed 6 November 2004).

9. "A Digest of California's Political Demography," *California Opinion Index*, January 2002, 7.

10. Derived from data in *Statement of Vote, 2002 General Election* (Sacramento: Secretary of State, 2002), vii.

11. Michael McDonald, "Voter Turnout," *United States Elections Project*, (n.d.) *http://elections.gmu.edu/Voter_Turnout_2002.htm* (accessed 6 November 2004).

12. "Voting in the 1994 General Election," *California Opinion Index*, January 1995, 2; "Digest of California's Political Demography," *California Opinion Index,* January 2002, 8.

13. Pacheco became governor in 1875 when Newton Booth resigned that position to become a U.S. senator.

14. James Fay and Kay Lawson, "Is California Going Republican?" in Maureen Moakley, ed., *Party Realignment and State Politics* (Columbus: Ohio State University Press, 1992), 17–34. See also "Political Demography," *California Opinion Index*, November 1992, 4.

15. Analysis by author. Data on assembly elections include uncontested races. Note that the Democrats' share of the votes is substantially less than its almost two-thirds control of assembly seats. This "bonus" of seats over votes for the majority party is typical in winner-take-all electoral systems. For a brief explanation of this phenomenon, see Roger H. Davidson and Walter J. Oleszek, *Congress and Its Members*, 7th ed. (Washington, D.C.: Congressional Quarterly Press, 2000), 59–61.

16. "Leaners" were counted as independents. Unmarried includes "divorced or separated," "living together," and "never married"; widowed respondents were excluded from the analysis. "Some college" includes vocational and technical school. "Latino" includes all respondents self-identifying as Hispanic regardless of race. Except for Hispanics, those identifying with more than one race were excluded from the analysis. Except for age, all relationships shown are statistically significant.

17. On the 1988 ruling, see Carl Ingram, "State's Campaign Funds Law Voided by Federal Judge," *Los Angeles Times,* 7 January 1998. The earlier ruling was handed down in the middle of the 1990 election campaigns. For a discussion of its impact on the 1990 gubernatorial race, see Gerald C. Lubenow, ed., *The 1990 Governor's Race: An Inside Look at the Candidates and Their Campaigns by the People Who Managed Them* (Berkeley: Institute of Governmental Studies, 1991), 157, 181ff. At the same time that voters approved Proposition 73, they also approved by a

narrower margin Proposition 68. This measure included both contribution limits and public financing. Because not all provisions of the competing Proposition 73 had been ruled unconstitutional, the California Supreme Court invalidated Proposition 68 in 1993. See Bob Egelko, "A Low Profile Court," *California Journal*, June 1994, 38.

18. Secretary of State, "Cal-Access: California Summary Data Report," (2 August, 2004) *http://dbsearch.ss.ca.gov/CandidateSummary.aspx* (accessed 2 August 2004).

19. Christian Berthelsen, "$80 Million in Contributions in 75-Day Recall Campaign," *San Francisco Chronicle*, 11 October 2003. On the impact of Proposition 34 generally, see, for example, Daniel Weintraub, "Campaign Finance Limits Feel Good but Don't Do Good," *Sacramento Bee*, 17 January 2002.

20. David McCuan, Shaun Bowler, Todd Donovan, and Ken Hernandez, "California's Political Warriors: Campaign Professionals and the Initiative Process," in Shaun Bowler, Todd Donovan, and Caroline J. Tolbert, eds., *Citizens as Legislators: Direct Democracy in the United* States (Columbus: Ohio State University Press, 1998), 27–54.

21. Mark Z. Barabek, "When Advisors Defect, the Rules Are Left Behind," *Los Angeles Times*, 11 April 1998.

22. "American Association of Political Consultants," *http://www.theaapc.com* (accessed 29 June 2000). The District of Columbia ranks a distant second to California in membership. Among the states Virginia, probably because of its proximity to D.C., ranks highest after California.

23. McCuan et al., "California's Political Warriors"; Susan Rasky, "Clem Whitaker and Leone Baxter," *California Journal*, November 1999, 50–51; Richard Rapaport, "In the Beginning: A History of California Political Consulting," *California Journal*, September 1991, 418–424; David Lee Rosenbloom, *The Election Men* (New York: Quadrangle, 1977), 45.

6. The State Legislature

1. As quoted in Sherry Bebitch Jeffe, "The Case of the Incredible Shrinking Legislature," *Los Angeles Times*, 20 June 2004.

2. From 1926 until 1972 California law did provide for a reapportionment commission to draw up district boundaries should the legislature fail to act. The commission remained dormant until 1971. Late that year, with the legislature and Governor Reagan deadlocked, Lieutenant Governor Ed Reinecke in his capacity as Reapportionment Commission chair convened the commission. Before it could act, the California Supreme Court invalidated the section of the state constitution that had established the commission. See "Reapportionment Reels Toward the Court as Republicans Deadlock Democrats," *California Journal*, December 1971, 328–329, 347–348; "Supreme Court Rules Against Reapportionment Plans, Reapportionment Commission," *California Journal*, January 1972, 7–8.

3. Peter Savodnik, "GOPers Fight Redistricting Reform: Calif. Members Take Early Stand Against Initiative," *The Hill*, 1 April 2004.

4. For a brief explanation of this phenomenon, see Roger H. Davidson and Walter J. Oleszek, *Congress and Its Members*, 7th ed. (Washington, D.C.: Congressional Quarterly Press, 2000), 59–61.

5. Author's analysis of preliminary data from Secretary of State, "California General Election, November 2, 2004," (5 November 2004) *http://vote2004.ss.ca.gov/Returns/ stasm/all.htm* (accessed 5 November 2004).

6. Daniel Weintraub, "The Story Behind the Democrats' Losing Streak," *Sacramento Bee*, 11 March 2004.

7. Citizens Conference on State Legislatures, *State Legislatures: An Analysis of Their Effectiveness* (New York: Praeger, 1971), 40.

8. Martin Smith, "The Rise and Decline of the California Legislature," in Gerald C. Lubenow and Bruce E. Cain, eds., *Governing California: Politics, Government, and Public Policy in the Golden State* (Berkeley: Institute of Governmental Studies, 1997), 4. A similar view is expressed in Charles Mahtesian, "The Sick Legislature Syndrome and How to Avoid it," in Thad L. Beyle, ed., *State Government 1997–98* (Washington, D.C.: Congressional Quarterly Press, 1997), 86–87.

9. "Summary and Citations of State Term Limit Laws," *National Conference of State Legislatures*, (5 May 2004) *http://www.ncsl.org/programs/legman/about/citations.htm* (accessed 6 November 2004).

10. Based on information in Stephen Green, ed., *California Political Almanac 1991–1992*, 2nd ed. (Sacramento: California Journal, 1991), *passim*. Averages are medians. Seats listed as vacant in the *Almanac* were not included in the calculations.

11. In a discussion of "electoral opportunity structures," Gary F. Moncrief, Peverill Squire, and Malcolm E. Jewell point out that the ratio of state legislative seats to statewide and federal elective offices is much lower in California than in most states and that this helps give rise in California to "progressive" career ambitions. See *Who Runs for the Legislature* (Upper Saddle River, N.J.: Prentice Hall, 2001), 23–24.

12. Membership information is from the assembly and senate Web sites at *http://www. assembly.ca.gov* and *http://www.senate.ca.gov*, and from the *Almanac of California Government and Politics*, 7th ed. (Sacramento: California Journal Press, 1989), 39–65.

13. Data on racial and ethnic population by district are from "Census 2000 Race Variables by 2001 District" *Statewide Database* (19 December 2001) *http://swdb. berkeley.edu/info/census2000/P002_by_2kDistrict.html* (accessed 6 November 2004).

14. Daniel Weintraub, "Moving Beyond Stereotypes in the Legislature," *Sacramento Bee*, 7 December 2000.

15. Lou Cannon, *Ronnie and Jesse: A Political Odyssey* (Garden City, N.Y.: Doubleday, 1969), 9–13, 21, 106–113; James R. Mills, *A Disorderly House: The Brown-Unruh Years in Sacramento* (Berkeley: Heyday Books, 1987), 31–46.

16. After a character by the same name in the play by Tennessee Williams, *Cat on a Hot Tin Roof* (Mills, *A Disorderly House*, 11; Cannon, *Ronnie and Jesse*, 109).

17. Richard A. Clucas, *The Speaker's Electoral Connection: Willie Brown and the California Assembly* (Berkeley: Institute of Governmental Studies, 1995), 14. There is

some disagreement as to just how powerful the speaker's position was prior to Unruh. Writing just before Unruh became speaker, *Time* magazine called it "a post that by the nature of its duties stands second only to the governorship in importance." See "Big Daddy," *Time,* 5 May 1961, 19. Clucas, however, writes that, before Unruh transformed the office, the speaker was "at best . . . only one of several important players in the legislature."

18. For a list of speakers up to Brown, see E. Dotson Wilson and Brian S. Ebbert, *California's Legislature* (Sacramento: California Assembly, 2000), 248–250.
19. James Richardson, *Willie Brown: A Biography* (Berkeley: University of California, 1996), 3–15, 40–41, 255–271.
20. Clucas, *The Speaker's Electoral Connection,* 1.
21. *Ibid.,* especially Chap. 3.
22. Leonard Roy Frank, ed., *Random House Webster's Quotationary* (New York: Random House, 1998), 619.
23. "Big Daddy," 20.
24. Clucas, *The Speaker's Electoral Connection,* 50ff.
25. For a more in-depth telling of the story that follows, see Richardson, *Willie Brown,* 374–382.
26. "Standing Rules of the Assembly, 2003–04 Regular Session," *California Assembly,* sects. 12 and 13 (2 December 2002) *http://www.leginfo.ca.gov/rules/assembly_rules.html* (accessed 6 November 2004).
27. Dan Walters, "The Decline of Committees," *Sacramento Bee,* 18 June 1999.
28. Roger H. Davidson and Walter J. Oleszek, *Congress and Its Members,* 9th ed. (Washington, D.C.: Congressional Quarterly Press, 2004), 203ff.
29. Daniel Weintraub, "California Insider," (13 August 2001) *http://www.sacbee.com/static/weblogs/insider/* (e-mail received 6 August 2001); *California Government Code,* sects. 85301(a) and 85305.
30. California Senate, "Senate Rules Text," sect. 11 (19 May 2004) *http://www.leginfo.ca.gov/rules/senate_rules.html* (accessed 6 November 2004).
31. Dan Walters, "Prop. 45's Defeat Sets Up Intense Competition for Senate's Top Spot," *Sacramento Bee,* 15 March, 2002.
32. Jordan Rau and Dan Morain, "Senate Democrats Choose Perata," *Los Angeles Times* (25 August 2004).
33. William K. Muir, Jr., *Legislature: California's School for Politics* (Chicago: University of Chicago Press, 1982), 58. For fuller descriptions of "the author system," see *ibid.,* Chapter 3, and George S. Blair and Houston I. Flournoy, *Legislative Bodies in California* (Belmont, Calif.: Dickenson, 1967), 27–29.
34. The scores were derived by combining ratings of legislative roll call voting in 2003 by four interest groups: the California Chamber of Commerce (24 October 2003) *http://www.calchamber.com/documents/03voterecord.pdf* (accessed 6 November 2004), the California Taxpayers' Association (21 January 2004) *http://www.caltax.org/Scorecard.Report.2003.pdf* (accessed 6 November 2004), the California Public Interest Research Group (Summer 2004) *http://calpirg.org/Scorecards/2003StateScorecard.pdf*

(accessed 6 November 2004) , and the American Association of University Women—California, (n.d.) *http://www.aauw-ca.org/policy/03votingrecord.htm* (accessed 6 November 2004). The composite measure was created for each chamber by extracting the first principle component produced by a factor analysis of the four measures, deriving factor scores, and scaling the results so that they ranged from 0 to 100. The first principle component accounted for 97 percent of total variance in both the assembly and the senate.

35. The members of the Moderate Caucus are listed in Robert Salladay, "'Mod Squad' of Democrats Reins in Assembly Liberal," *Los Angeles Times*, 9 June 2004, while the membership of the Democratic Study Group can be found in California Teachers Association, "Coalition Urges Holdouts to Support Pending Budget Plan," *Politics and Legislation* (22 June 2003) *http://www.cta.org/PoliticsandLegislation/ePAL/v15n10/v15n10_coalition.htm* (accessed 6 November 2004).

36. There seems to be no single analysis that covers the period in question systematically, but the overall pattern can be pieced together by combining a variety of sources: William Buchanan, *Legislative Partisanship: The Deviant Case of California,* vol. 13 of *University of California Publications in Political Science* (Berkeley: University of California Press, 1963); Barbara J. Burt, "The California Legislature: Consensus and Conflict on Energy Policy in the 1970s" (paper presented at the annual meeting of the Western Political Science Association, Las Vegas, Nevada, 1985); Barbara J. Burt, "Policy Voting in the California Legislature 1975–82" (paper presented at the annual meeting of the American Political Science Association, Washington, D.C., 1986); Malcolm E. Jewell and Samuel C. Patterson, *The Legislative Process in the United States,* 1st–3d eds. (New York: Random House, 1966, 1973, 1977), 420–421 [1966], 445–446 [1973], and 384–385 [1977]; H. L. LeBlanc, "Voting in State Senates: Party and Constituency Influences," *Midwest Journal of Political Science* 13 (February 1969): 33–52; Donald Neil McIsaac, Jr., "Statistical Analysis of California Legislative Voting Blocs," (Ph.D. diss., Claremont Graduate School, 1966); John R. Owens, Edmond Costantini, and Louis E. Weschler, *California Politics and Parties* (New York: Macmillan, 1970), 317–320; Charles Marshall Price, "Voting in the California Legislature: A Roll Call Analysis of the 1957–59–61 Sessions," (Ph.D. diss., University of Southern California, 1965); Bruce W. Robeck, "Legislative Partisanship, Constituency, and Malapportionment: The Case of California," *American Political Science Review* 66 (December 1972): 1246–1255.

37. Robert J. Pitchell, "The Electoral System and Voting Behavior: The Case of California's Cross-Filing," *Western Political Quarterly* 12 (June 1959): 459–484.

38. Robeck, "Legislative Partisanship, Constituency, and Malapportionment."

39. Clucas, *The Speaker's Electoral Connection,* 66–69.

40. "2003 Legislator Compensation," *National Conference of State Legislatures,* (2004) *http://www.ncsl.org/programs/legman/03Table-legcomp.htm* (accessed 6 November 2004).

41. Peverill Squire, "Uncontested Seats in State Legislative Elections," *Legislative Studies Quarterly* 25 (February 2000): 135, 142–143.

7. The State's Plural Executive

1. As quoted by Alan Greenblatt, "Strong Governor," *Governing*, July 2004, 28.
2. Thad L. Beyle, "Gubernatorial Power: The Institutional Power Ratings for the 50 Governors of the United States," (3 March 2003) *http://www.unc.edu/~beyle/gubnewpwr.html* (accessed 31 October 2004).
3. The office of insurance commissioner differs from other elected state executive positions in that it was created by statute rather than by the state constitution. For this reason, it is not covered by the term-limit provisions of Proposition 140. The office is, however, limited to two terms by statute.
4. *The Book of the States 2004* (Lexington, Ky.: Council of State Governments, 2004), 173–174.
5. John Jacobs, "The Governor: Managing a Mega-State," in Gerald C. Lubenow and Bruce E. Cain, eds., *Governing California: Politics, Government, and Public Policy in the Golden State* (Berkeley: Institute of Governmental Studies, 1997), 37–38.
6. California Constitution, art. IV, sect. 10.
7. Jon Matthews, "Wilson Dodges Override," *Pasedena Star News*, 4 March 1994; Larry N. Gerston, "'Gov. No' Rules Sacramento in a Hail of Vetoes," *Los Angeles Times* 11 July 2001.
8. California Constitution, art. IV, sect. 10.
9. *The Book of the States 2004,* 162–163.
10. This includes William Irwin, governor from 1875 until 1880, who had served as acting lieutenant governor, but who had not been elected to that post. See E. Dotson Wilson and Brian S. Ebbert, *California's Legislature* (Sacramento: California State Assembly, 2000), 237–238.
11. California Constitution, art. IX, sect. 9.
12. *Ibid.*, art. V, sect. 10.
13. Patrick Hoge, "Quackenbush Steps Down: Insurance Chief Target of Several State Probes," *Sacramento Bee,* 29 June 2000.
14. For example, a Field Poll of likely voters conducted just prior to the 1998 general election showed that, among those registered as either Democrats or Republicans, 66 percent voted in a manner consistent with their registration; in the seven partisan statewide executive races that year, the same poll showed a rate of voting consistent with major party registration that ranged from 75 to 88 percent (or 78 to 91 percent when only votes for major party candidates were considered). (Author's analysis of October 22–November 1, 1998 Field Poll.)
15. Deborah Anderluh, "Low-Profile Race for Schools Chief: Superintendent's Authority Cut," *Sacramento Bee,* 19 May 1998.
16. John Jacobs, "Angelides Understands Money and Public Policy," *Sacramento Bee,* 4 April 1999.
17. *Ibid.*
18. Full-time equivalent positions. U.S. Bureau of the Census, "State Government Employment Data: California," (March 2002) *http://ftp2.census.gov/govs/apes/02stca.txt* (accessed 31 October 2004).

19. *Governor's Budget 2004–2005* (Sacramento: Department of Finance, 2004), LJE 19.

20. Gary G. Hamilton and Nicole Woolsey Biggart, *Governor Reagan, Governor Brown: A Sociology of Executive Power* (New York: Columbia University Press, 1984), 62–64; Nicole Woolsey Biggart, *The Magic Circle: A Study of Personal Staffs in the Administrations of Governors Ronald Reagan and Jerry Brown* (Ph.D. diss., University of California, Berkeley, 1981), 40.

21. Paul Jacobs, "Spill Poses Immediate Challenge for New Cal/EPA," *Los Angeles Times*, 18 July 1991.

22. Greg King, *Deliver Us from Evil. A Public History of California's Civil Service System* (Sacramento: Office of Planning and Research, State of California, 1979), 3–6.

23. *Ibid.*, 25–29.

24. *Ibid.*, 21–22.

25. *Ibid.*, 52.

26. Bruce Hackett, *Higher Civil Servants in California* (Berkeley and Davis: Institute for Governmental Studies and Institute for Governmental Affairs, 1979), 69–70.

27. *Ibid.*, 67–68. See also John Birkenstock, Ronald Kurtz, and Steven Phillips, "Career Executive Assignments—Report on a California Innovation," *Public Personnel Management* 4 (May–June 1975): 151–155; John F. Fisher and Robert J. Erickson, "California Career Executive Assignment: I. Meeting the Challenge for Better Managers," *Public Personnel Review* 25 (April 1964): 82–86; Lloyd D. Musolf, "California Career Executive Assignment: II. A Perilous But Necessary Voyage," *Public Personnel Review* 25 (April 1964): 87–89.

28. Biggart, *The Magic Circle*, 42.

29. Hackett, *Higher Civil Servants in California*, 67.

30. *CCRC News* (Sacramento: California Constitution Revision Commission, May 1996).

31. Christian Berthelsen, Lynda Gledhill, John M. Hubbell, and Victoria Colliver, "Governor Looks Beyond Budget, Plans Big Government Overhaul," *San Francisco Chronicle*, 30 July 2004; Peter Nicholas and Robert Salladay, "Radical Revamp of State Bureaucracy," *Los Angeles Times*, 20 July 2004.

32. Evan Halper, "Plan Won't Fix Budget, Analyst Says," *Los Angeles Times*, 28 August 2004.

33. Jordan Rau, "The Savings Bump Up Against the Costs," *Los Angeles Times*, 31 July 2004.

8. The Judicial Process

1. *Democracy in America*, tr. Harvey C. Mansfield and Delba Winthrop (Chicago: University of Chicago Press, 2000 [1835, 1840]), 257

2. Based on data from U.S. Bureau of the Census, ""Table NST-EST2003-01—Annual Estimates of the Population for the United States and States, and for Puerto Rico: April 1, 2000 to July 1, 2003" (18 December 2003) *http://www.census.gov/popest/ states/tables/NST-EST2003-01.pdf* (accessed 31 October 2004) and American Bar Association, "National Lawyer Population by State," (2004) *http://www.abanet.org/ marketresearch/2004nbroflawyersbystate.pdf* (accessed 31 October 2004).

3. California Constitution, art. III, sect. 5; art. IX, sect. 12.

4. As of June 30, 2003. Judicial Council of California, *2004 Court Statistics Report* (San Francisco: Administrative Office of the Courts, 2004), 60.1–60.2.

5. California Constitution, art. VI, sect. 22; Judicial Council of California, "California Rules of Court, Rule 6.609," (1 January 2002) *http://www.courtinfo.ca.gov/rules/ titlesix/titlesix.pdf* (accessed 31 October 2004).

6. Judicial Council of California, "California Courts Make History as Last County Unifies Trial Courts Today," (8 February 2001) *http://www.courtinfo.ca.gov/ newsreleases/NR14-01.HTM* (accessed 31 October 2004).

7. Marianne Jameson, "The Grand Jury: A Brief Historical Overview," *California Grand Jurors' Association*, (n.d.) *http://www.nvo.com/cgja/nss-folder/briefhistoryofgrandjuries/ Grdjry.rtf* (accessed 31 October 2004). In addition to its role in criminal cases described here, the grand jury also serves as a local government "watchdog."

8. California Penal Code, sect. 904.6.

9. California Grand Jurors' Association, "2001 California Grand Jury Practices Survey," (November 2001) *http://www.nvo.com/cgja/nss-folder/onlinepublications2/survey.pdf* (accessed 31 October 2004).

10. Bruce T. Olson, *Grand Juries in California: A Study in Citizenship* (Modesto, Calif.: American Grand Jury Association, 2000), 83.

11. California Grand Jurors' Association, "2001 California Grand Jury Practices Survey."

12. California Constitution, Art. XI, sects. 1(b) and 4(c).

13. California Public Defenders Association, "Draft Survey Results—2003 Defender Office Staffing Levels by County, State, and Federal for California," (February 2003) *http://www.cpda.org/DefenderStaffingLevels/2003-Survey-Statewide-Defender-Office-Staffing.pdf* (accessed 9 July 2004).

14. A third type of jury is the coroner's jury. Such juries are occasionally convened by the coroner to assist in determining the cause of a death. California Government Code, sects. 27491.6, 27492–27497, 27504, 68095. See also Cortus T. Koehler, *Managing California's Counties: Serving People, Solving Problems* (Sacramento: County Supervisors Association of California, 1983), 101.

15. California Constitution, art. I, sect. 16; California Code of Civil Procedure, sect. 220.

16. California Constitution, art. I, sect. 16.

17. Judicial Council of California, *2004 Court Statistics Report*, 55.

18. *Ibid.*, 51, 55, 56.

19. Preble Stolz, "The California Supreme Court," in Gerald C. Lubenow and Bruce E. Cain, eds., *Governing California: Politics, Government, and Public Policy in the Golden State* (Berkeley: Institute of Governmental Studies, 1997), 45. Appeals by the prosecution on procedural rulings are permitted. See California Penal Code, sect. 1238.

20. Appellate Defenders, Inc., "Appellate Projects in California," (2004) *http://www. adi-sandiego.com/Resources/Addresses/projects_address.htm* (accessed 31 October 2004).

21. Judicial Council of California, *2004 Court Statistics Report*, 27, 28.

22. Judicial Council of California, "What Appellate Justices Do," California Courts: The Judicial Branch of California 2004, *http://www.courtinfo.ca.gov/courts/ courtsofappeal/3rdDistrict/do.htm* (accessed 31 October 2004).

23. Judicial Council of California, *2004 Court Statistics Report*, 8.

24. Maura Dolan, "Signs Point to Rifts on State High Court," *Los Angeles Times*, 4 December 2000.

25. Excluded from the analysis presented here was *Alford v. Superior Court*, 29 Cal. 4th 1033 (2003) because the court was divided three ways, with no clear majority. In all other cases, justices were coded as in agreement even when they issued separate opinions dissenting in whole or in part from the majority and may, therefore, not have been in less than complete accord with one another.

26. Dolan, "Signs Point to Rifts on State High Court"; Maura Dolan, "Chief Justice Seen as More Independent," *Los Angeles Times*, 30 January 2001.

27. Dolan, "Signs Point to Rifts on State High Court"; Maura Dolan, "Disorder on the Court Comes Out in the Record," *Los Angeles Times*, 4 December 2000.

28. California Constitution, art. VI, sect. 6.

29. The Judicial Council's Working Group on Judicial Selection, "Report on ACA 1 (Nation): Superior Court Elections," (7 June 2001) *http://www.courtinfo.ca.gov/ reference/documents/aca1wgr.pdf* (accessed 31 October 2004).

30. Stolz, "California's Supreme Court," 50n.

31. Preble Stolz, *Judging Judges: The Investigation of Rose Bird and the California Supreme Court* (New York: Free Press, 1981).

32. California Constitution, art. VI, sects. 8, 18.

33. *Ibid.* In June 1998, voters further amended the constitution to give the commission authority to discipline subordinate judicial officers. See also *California Supplemental Voter Pamphlet, General Election, Nov. 8, 1994*, 18–20.

34. State of California Commission on Judicial Performance, "Public Discipline/ Dismissals—1960 to Present," (n.d.) *http://www.cjp.ca.gov/pubdisc.htm* (accessed 31 October 2004).

35. For guidance in the research for this section, the author is greatly indebted to his colleague, Prof. Douglas Glaeser.

36. In the mid-1970s, the California Supreme Court was sharply divided on the merits of relying on the "independent grounds" doctrine. See Ronald Blubaugh, "A Philosophical Struggle Within the Supreme Court," *California Journal*, November 1984, 382–384; and Ronald Blubaugh, "The State Supreme Court's Declaration of Independence," *California Journal*, May 1976, 153–154.

37. *People v. Brisendine* 13 Cal. 3d 528, 549–550 (1975).

38. California Constitution, art. I, sect. 24.

39. *Jankovich v. Toll Road Commission* 379 U.S. 487, 491–492 (1965).

40. *Pruneyard Shopping Center v. Robins* 447 U.S. 74 (1980).

41. *Lloyd Corp. v. Tanner* 407 U.S. 551, 567 (1972).

42. *Robins v. Pruneyard Shopping Center* 23 Cal. 3d 899 (1979).

43. California Constitution, art. I, sect. 2, reads in part: "Every person may freely speak, write and publish his or her sentiments on all subjects. . . ." Art. I, sect. 3, reads, "the people have the right to instruct their representatives, petition government for redress of grievances, and assemble freely to consult for the common good."

44. Paige M. Harrison and Jennifer C. Karberg, "Prison and Jail Inmates at Midyear 2003." *Bureau of Justice Statistics Bulletin* (May 2004) *http://www.ojp.usdoj.gov/bjs/pub/pdf/pjim03.pdf* (accessed 31 October 2004).

45. California Youth Authority, "Step Inside the CYA," (2000) *http://www.cya.ca.gov/* (accessed 31 October 2004).

46. "Crime in California, 2002," 77 (n.d.) *http://ag.ca.gov/cjsc/publications/candd/cd02/cdintro.htm* (accessed 31 October 2004).

47. John Howard, "A New Look at Crime and Punishment," *California Journal*, May 2004, 11–12.

48. "Monthly Report of Population" (6 July 2004) *http://www.corr.ca.gov/OffenderInfo Services/Reports/Monthly/TPOP1A/TPOP1Ad0406.pdf* (accessed 31 October 2004).

49. Jenifer Warren, "Takeover of State Prisons Is Threatened," *Los Angeles Times*, 21 July 2004.

50. *California Voter Voter Pamphlet, General Election, Nov. 8, 1994*, 34.

9. Local Government

1. René DuBos, *Celebrations of Life* (New York: McGraw-Hill, 1983), 83.

2. Leonard Roy Frank, ed., *Random House Webster's Quotationary* (New York: Random House, 1998), 619.

3. D. J. Waldie, "Phantom Governments," *Los Angeles Times,* 4 June 2000.

4. U.S. Census Bureau, "Annual Estimates of the Population in Incorporated Places Over 100,000," (24 June 2004) *http://www.census.gov/popest/cities/tables/SUB-EST2003-01.pdf* (accessed 31 October 2004).

5. Here and elsewhere, except as indicated, population estimates for cities and counties are from the *California Statistical Abstract, 2003* (Sacramento: Department of Finance, 2003), 14ff. Figures are as of 1 January 2003.

6. *California Government Code,* sect. 56000 et seq.; Owen Newcomer, *Governing Los Angeles* (New York: McGraw-Hill, 1993), 44.

7. *Cities Annual Report, Fiscal Year 2001–02* (Sacramento: State Controller, 2004), xx.

8. *Ibid.*, 7–12.

9. California Constitution, art. XI, sect. 3.

10. *Municipal Yearbook, 1987* (Washington, D.C.: International City/County Management Association, 1987), 180–183.

11. *Ibid.*

12. California Government Code, sect. 36516.

13. *Municipal Yearbook, 2004* (Washington, D.C.: International City/County Management Association, 2004), 198–202.

14. *Compensation 2004* (Washington, D.C.: ICMA, 2004), 114–122. Figures include some unincorporated towns.

15. Pearson's r = .61.

16. John Taylor, "Overview," *California Association of Counties,* (n.d.) *http://www.csac.counties.org/default.asp?id=52* (accessed 31 October 2004).

17. County of Los Angeles, "Overview," (n.d.) *http://lacounty.info/overview.htm* (accessed 31 October 2004).

18. *Counties Annual Report, Fiscal Year 2000–2001* (Sacramento: State Controller, 2003), xiii, xvi, 6–13. The categories used here include both enterprise activities and general financing.

19. *Ibid.*, 1.

20. California Institute of County Government, "Supervisor Compensation Survey Data," (11 May 2001) *http://cicg.org/publications/supsal_table.htm* (accessed 31 October 2004).

21. California Constitution, art. XI, sects. l and 4.

22. *Municipal Yearbook, 2004,* 285.

23. *Compensation 2004*, 258–259.

24. Education Data Partnership, "Fiscal, Demographic, and Performance Data on California's K-12 Schools," (12 May 2004) *http://www.ed-data.k12.ca.us* (accessed 31 October 2004); *California Statistical Abstract 2003* (Sacramento: Department of Finance, 2003), 107.

25. California Postsecondary Education Commission, "California Community College Information," (2004) *http://www.cpec.ca.gov/CollegeGuide/CCCSystemInformation. asp* (accessed 31 October 2004).

26. *California Voter Information Guide Ballot Pamphlet: Primary Election, June 2, 1998* (Sacramento: Secretary of State, 1998), 32.

27. Except where indicated otherwise, information in this section is from *Special Districts Annual Report, Fiscal Year 1996–1997* (Sacramento: State Controller, 1999); *Special Districts Annual Report, Fiscal Year 2001–2002* (Sacramento: State Controller, 2004); and the Little Hoover Commission "Special Districts: Relics of the Past or Resources for the Future?" (3 May 2000) *http://www.lhc.ca.gov/lhcdir/155/ report155.pdf* (accessed 31 October 2004).

28. *Salyer Land Co. v. Tulare Water District*, 410 U.S. 719 (1973).

29. Little Hoover Commission, "Special Districts," iv, 17.

30. *Ibid.*, 18ff.

31. Secretary of State, "Initiatives" (5 May 2003) *http://www.ss.ca.gov/elections/elections_ initiatives.htm* (accessed 31 October 2004).

32. The Elections Code also provides for the indirect initiative at the county level, but, if any such measures were approved during the period reported here, they were not included in the Secretary of State's tabulations.

33. Based on data from the California State University, Sacramento Institute for Social Research, "Data Files and Reports Available: California Elections Data Archive" (2 July 2003) *http://www.csus.edu/isr/isr3.html* (accessed 14 July 2004).

34. City of Lakewood, "The Lakewood Plan," (2002) *http://www.lakewoodcity.org/info/ community/lakewood_history/lakewood_plan.asp* (accessed 31 October 2004).

35. California Contract Cities Association, "CCAA Listing by City," (n.d.) *http://www. contractcities.org/pages/about_us/member_cities.asp* (accessed 31 October 2004).

36. J. S. Taub, "COGs' Failures as Regional Planners: COGs Search for a New Mission," *California Journal*, November 1986, 551–554.

37. Governor's Office of Planning and Research, "Directory of California's Councils of Government," *The California Planners' Book of Lists 2000*, (n.d.) *http://ceres.ca.gov/planning/bol/2000/cog.html* (accessed 14 July 2004).
38. Taub, "COGs' Failures as Regional Planners."
39. *CCRC News* (Sacramento: California Constitution Revision Commission, May 1996).
40. Steven L. Pevar, "State Power Over Indian Affairs," in *The Rights of Indians and Tribes: The Authoritative ACLU Guide to Indian and Tribal Rights*, 3rd ed. (Carbondale: Southern Illinois University Press, 2002), 119–141.
41. California State Association of Counties, "Fact Sheet on Indian Gaming in California" (5 November 2003) *http://www.csac.counties.org/legislation/indian_gaming/fact_sheet2.pdf* (accessed 29 August 2004).
42. The Confederation of American Indians, *Indian Reservations: A State and Federal Handbook* (Jefferson, N.C.: McFarland, 1986), 28–74.
43. *California Voter Information Guide, March 7, 2000 Primary Election* (Sacramento: Secretary of State, 2000), 4–5.
44. Louis Sahagun, "Casino Revives Tribe's Old Rivalries," *Los Angeles Times*, 16 February 2004.
45. David Plotz, "How Indians Took Over California Politics," *New Republic*, 13 March 2000, 29.
46. Bill Whalen, "The New Special Interest: Native American-run Gambling as a Big Money Political Player," *Campaigns and Elections*, July 2004, 20.
47. Joel Rubin, "Bloodlines Issue Divides Tribe," *Los Angeles Times*, 30 November 2003; Sahagun, "Casino Revives Tribe's Old Rivalries"; Louis Sahagun, "Pechanga Band Ousts Scores of Tribal Members," *Los Angeles Times*, 20 March 2004; Michael Hiltzik, "Fairness Is the Loser in Tribal Identity Crisis," *Los Angeles Times*, 5 April 2004.
48. *California Voter Information Guide, November 2, 2004 General Election* (Sacramento: Secretary of State, 2004), 54, 64.

10. Financing California Government

1. "Taxes and Government Spending," *California Opinion Index*, December 2001.
2. David Bowman et al., "Structural Deficit and the Long-Term Fiscal Condition of the State," in John J. Kerlin and Jeffrey I. Chapman, eds., *California Policy Choices*, vol. 9 (Los Angeles: University of Southern California School of Public Administration, 1994), 47.
3. Based on data in "Federal, State, and Local Governments: State and Local Government Finances," (16 July 2004) *http://www.census.gov/govs/www/estimate.html* (accessed 4 August, 2004) and "Annual State Personal Income," (April 2004) *http://www.bea.doc.gov/bea/regional/spi/* (accessed 4 August 2004). Figures are for "general" revenues and expenditures and exclude such things as utility, liquor, and insurance trust revenues and expenditures, and outstanding debt. The term "general" is avoided in order to prevent confusion with the state's "general fund," a much narrower concept that is discussed later in the chapter.
4. Ranking calculated by this author from Robert S. McIntyre et al., *Who Pays? A Distributional Analysis of the Tax Systems in All 50 States* (Washington, D.C.: Institute

on Taxation and Economic Policy, 2003). The measure used is the ratio of state and local tax rates for the poorest 20 percent of the population to that for the top 1 percent, taking into account federal deductions for state and local taxes.

5. Scott A. Hodge, J. Scott Moody, and Wendy P. Warcholik, "State Business Climate Index," (May 2003) *http://www.taxfoundation.org/bp41.pdf* (accessed 5 August 2004).

6. *Governor's Budget May Revision 2004–05* (Sacramento: Department of Finance, 2004), 11.

7. For a useful summary of how ballot propositions have shaped and limited California's budget process, see "Ballot Box Budgeting: Budget-Related Propositions," *California Journal*, September 1997, 12–14.

8. John E. Petersen, "Going for Broke," *Governing*, March 2004, 70.

9. The legislature did eventually vote to place a property-tax-relief referendum on the ballot, but it was too little, too late, and went down to defeat.

10. *Economic Report of the Governor 1998* (Sacramento: Department of Finance, 1998), A–30.

11. "Prop. 13—Twenty Years Later," *California Opinion Index*, May 1998.

12. *California Ballot Pamphlet: General Election, November 5, 1996* (Sacramento: Secretary of State, 1996), 74.

13. Jeffrey L. Rabin, "Spending Cap in Place Already," *Los Angeles Times*, 27 November, 2003.

14. The definitive work on this subject is Richard Krolak, *California's Budget Dance: Issues and Process*, 2nd ed. (Sacramento: California Journal Press, 1994), Chaps. 4–6.

15. Robert Keith, "A Brief Introduction to the Federal Budget Process," (13 November 1996) *http://www.house.gov/rules/96-912.htm* (accessed 31 October 2004).

16. *Ibid.*

17. *California Constitution*, art. IV, sect. 12(a).

18. *2004–05 Governor's Budget Summary* (Sacramento: Department of Finance, 2004), A–14.

19. The estimate is by the California Budget Project, as cited in George Skelton, "Millions of Micro-Managers Share Blame for State's Crises," *Los Angeles Times*, 25 September 2003.

20. *2004–05 Governor's Budget Summary*, Schedules 8 and 9.

21. *State of California Cities Annual Report (Fiscal Year 2001–02)* (Sacramento: State Controller's Office, 27 May 2004), vi; *State of California Counties Annual Report (Fiscal Year 2001–02)* (Sacramento: State Controller's Office, 13 July 2004), v.

22. The precise figures for intergovernmental revenue (as a percent of total revenue) for cities are as follows: federal, 4.92%; state, 8.06%; county and other, 0.75%. The figures for counties are: federal, 22.36%; state, 39.92%; other, 1.25%.

23. *State of California Special Districts Annual Report (Fiscal Year 2001–02)* (Sacramento: State Controller's Office, 30 June 2004), viii.

24. *State of California School Districts Annual Report (Fiscal Year 1999–00)* (Sacramento: State Controller's Office, 30 July 2003), ix. Includes K–12 school districts, county boards of education, and joint powers authorities, but not community college districts.

Index